Zoe - T
support! I
enjoys it!

LONG STORYies
SHORTened

Go past the Dak, catch the San at the loop and cross the powerlines... into the slicks.

A collection of short stories and vignettes by
WILLIAM J PETERS

 **FriesenPress**

One Printers Way
Altona, MB R0G 0B0
Canada

www.friesenpress.com

Copyright © 2025 by William J Peters
First Edition — 2025

All rights reserved.

All rights reserved. No part of this publication may be reproduced, distributed or transmitted in any form or by any means, including photocopying, recording, or other electronic or mechanical methods, without the prior written permission of the author, except for brief quotations in critical reviews or noncommercial uses permitted by copyright law.

ISBN
978-1-03-833144-1 (Hardcover)
978-1-03-833143-4 (Paperback)
978-1-03-833145-8 (eBook)

1. BIOGRAPHY & AUTOBIOGRAPHY, PERSONAL MEMOIRS

Distributed to the trade by The Ingram Book Company

Table of Contents

ix	Acknowledgements
xi	Foreword
1	Ode (and owed) to Mom...
5	All you need to know about me
8	Z is for Zorro!
10	And the award goes to...
11	Minnetonka School
13	My Winnie Cooper
18	Catch the San at the loop, past the powerlines into the sticks
22	What'd you get?
26	Those summer days
28	The dog catcher
31	The devaluation of Coke
34	Dropmore memories
36	There's no place like home
39	One small step for man, one giant break for Dropmore squirrel
41	Mandingo!
43	Bush party busted
47	The goal
50	Breaking the ice
53	Robert Marvin "Bobby" Hull
57	Maurice "The Rocket" Richard
60	Bittersweet memories
65	Ladies with hats

66	The circle game
69	We were idiots
72	Sykotherapy
75	Community club dance
77	Ode to #4
78	Comedians in bars getting coffee
79	That time I almost killed a guy
83	Daily takeout
84	The real veal deal
85	Mary Tyler Moore
87	A brief eternity in Pine Falls
91	A Christmas tale
93	The value of a dream
95	The milkman
97	Calling in reinforcements
98	The nativity
100	Dr. John
104	Oh Henry
108	The Chrome Pit
110	Hit it!
111	White on rice
112	Yay sports!
113	Sorry Dr. King
114	Pawan K. Singal
117	Paging Dr. R.D. Weinberg
119	Father's Day, 2023
121	Chips and dip
122	Everything I needed to know
125	Changing of the season
126	Sweet, sweet chili
127	Into the breach

128	Another world
129	Just Vince
131	Things I learned from my dad
134	It's all white now
135	Moving the world
136	Being there
138	Off-Centre
140	"Whale hump"
141	Thoughts at -35°C
142	To everything a season
145	Getting my hands dirty
147	Oh chute
148	Godspeed Neil Peart
149	Uptown funk
150	No good deed
152	Lorne Robb, the "legend of Churchill"
156	Thoughts and prayers
157	The magic of Auntie Kay
161	The ring
164	God Bless the heroes
165	Crazy 'bout a Mercury
168	Remembering Constable John Constable
170	Testament to a friend, and a stranger
173	Essay: American Hitler
175	Lunch with POTUS
177	Darkness over a city of light
179	"Neither shall they learn war…"
181	A word from the fence
183	Father's Day
184	Seconds of terror
186	Paranoia

188	Red Friday
192	Dad's obit
196	Worst New Year's Eve. Ever.
198	On being famous
200	High school fight
202	Olivia's grip
205	Hacking (cough)
206	The physics of poop
208	Where's Christian?
209	Finding Jesus
211	Finding Jesus, Pt. 2
214	911 memorial
215	In a New York state of mind
217	Learning to help
220	Living through the kids
221	Making lemonade
224	My Robbie
227	Only waiting
228	Westminster chat
230	Young boy's dream
231	Squeeze your bum?
232	The secret to marriage
233	Mementos
234	Cheaper. Much cheaper.
235	Pawsh Tidy, please
236	Cars that can fly
237	Trunks of cars
238	Miss Universe
239	The ICONic last word from Stephen Eric McIntyre
241	About St. Amant
243	About the Author

Acknowledgements

There are a great many people responsible for the content of this book. Firstly, I'd like to acknowledge my parents, Bill and Irene Peters, who are responsible for my being; my siblings, Bonnie, Bob, Denise and Diane, for contextualizing my existence. My wife Roula, who puts up with me (this is harder than anyone can imagine), and Olivia and Christian, to whom all of the following was initially intended: I can't imagine life without you. You've given mine meaning.

Never underestimate what encouragement can do. This book would definitely not have been written without the encouragement of Mr. John Matthews, my Grade 8 and 9 Language Arts teacher, who challenged me to love reading. Nor would it have happened without Cheryl Liessens, who said *"You've always been a writer, Bill. You need to take this course (Red River College's Creative Communications). You'd be good at it."* Those were exactly the right words, at the right time.

Mr. Matthews and me

Cheryl and me

Special thanks as well to Juliette Mucha, Former Executive Director of St. Amant Foundation, and Les Wiens, long-time friend and author of *A Natural Cause,* for their support of this book!

"Dad, tell me a story."

When the kids were young, I used to read bedtime stories to them almost every night. We had lots of books, and after I'd read through them a few times they got boring – for me and the kids. So I started telling stories of growing up, playing sports, and going to school... pretty much anything I could think of. After a while I started thinking I should write some of them down, maybe produce a book of stories they could keep for the future. Something they could read to *their* kids. So I started writing. Five stories became ten. Then twenty. Then fifty. Then one hundred!

I put one of the stories online. *Catch the San at the Loop, past the Powerlines into the Sticks,* has since received almost 1,000 views. And from this I started receiving messages encouraging me to write a book. Alright already!

This is that book.

Foreword

Recounting these stories has been cathartic in so many ways. Walking literally and figuratively through the old neighbourhood has inspired so many memories, good and bad. Best of all, however, has been the hundreds of friends and acquaintances that have been resurrected in my mind, and consequently in many of my stories. Perhaps you will find yourself mentioned herein!

Celebrating 31 years together

Of course some of you are more obviously included by name, like my kids, Olivia and Christian. My wife Roula is of course contained herein, if she in fact can be contained. She is reluctantly here, as she has always contended that there is a way I can refer to her, simply, with suitable pronouns. It's easier just to call her Roula. And I will casually do so, as if you know her as well as I do. Not that anyone, especially I, can fully know or understand her, as she is, as Churchill once said, a riddle wrapped in an enigma. But he said that of Russia, and Roula is Greek. I've said too much. Sorry, I digress.

Of course my friends and most of my neighbours are in this book. They interacted with, and thus impacted me in various ways. So it should go without saying that my teachers are in this book as well – all of them. My pets through the years too, with Penny (best dog ever, God bless her), Puppy (the vengeful Chihuahua) and Luna the Wonder dog getting special mention. If only they could read...

Many others are also included by name. Childhood friend Cheryl was one of the first people I interviewed for accuracy regarding my early years, although I had to keep reminding her that I existed in her life too. My buddy Earl has listened to me, ad nauseam, running details of various and sundry memories from the past by him and asking questions like *"Can you believe Cheryl couldn't remember me giving her a pack of Juicy Fruit in Grade 4?* and *"Did you notice all we talk about are the girls we wished we'd asked out in high school?",* and *"So what have you got planned for today?"* As if retired people plan stuff...

Anyway, you're going to have to read this book to the end to see if you are mentioned by name. But the fact that you bothered to read this far... well, I thought of you many times as I wrote these stories. As much as these stories are to be a record of my life experiences and were initially intended for my kids (and perhaps their kids) to read, I hope I've managed to make them interesting to the wider audience that may not know me personally. My editors think so; hopefully you will as well.

During the process of writing this book, many have asked me about the details of financing (self-financed), writing (over several years), editing (thanks FriesenPress) and distribution (I don't know, door-to-door?), and mused about the proceeds (all proceeds go to St. Amant Foundation). At this point in my life I am comfortably retired, and am happy to support the St. Amant Foundation, as their Centre is a cornerstone of the neighbourhood I grew up in. And they continue to do amazing and necessary work supporting people with developmental disabilities, autism and acquired brain injury in our community! You can find out more about them at **stamant.ca**

Ode (and owed) to Mom...

I have the great good fortune of being able to get together for coffee regularly with my 87-year-old mom, and we often discuss this book.

"You know, I've been reviewing the manuscript and I realized there are no stories specifically about you" I said. "Not that you are not in the book, but the stories you are in tend to focus on other things. And there are a few Dad stories, so the imbalance kind of bothers me".

"That's fine," she replied. Her response did not come as a surprise. From the very beginning of our family, Mom has played a supporting role. She has been, and still is, there for all of us. "But I probably could have been a better mother." What??!!

Mom's family hails from Dropmore, Manitoba (pop. 80 or so), where her father, William Roy Robb, was the town's grain elevator operator. Her siblings, in order of birth, were Alvin, Kathleen (Kay), and twins Laurence and Clarence. Mom was the last of them, three years younger than the twins and a full 10 years younger than her sister Kay. Her mother, Agnes Mary Robb, had her at the relatively advanced age of 44 and was sick, often bedridden, since mom was four. Mom recalls caring for her mother during the day from age four when her siblings were in school, though her father was a few hundred yards away at the local grain elevator and could be called upon to help if needed. Kay, being the oldest female sibling, instinctively took over the kitchen, and shooed mom out when she offered to help. At 17, she taught in a one-room school house for a year, but when her dad retired in 1953 the family moved to Winnipeg. Mom was in her late teens then, and beyond the teaching stint had very little life experience. And almost zero kitchen or cooking experience.

Dad grew up on a farm a mile and a half north of Plum Coulee, very much in the Mennonite tradition. His first language was Low German; he learned to speak English and German in school, which he attended until he finished Grade 8. His siblings included seven brothers and two sisters. He left the farm to work for the telegraphs in Fort William, Ontario, but soon moved to Winnipeg when lineman jobs opened up at Winnipeg Hydro. He was a scrupulous and determined saver, and though he managed to buy a small house on Riviera Crescent in Fort Garry, he rented it out and lived with his brother Pete and sister-in-law Katie. As fate would have it, they lived next door to the Robb's, and Dad immediately had eyes for the beautiful 18-year old girl that lived there. Despite being told by his brothers that she was *way* out of his league, Dad married Mom in 1956 and they moved in to the Riviera Crescent house. Bonnie was born to them in 1958, and I followed in February of 1960. By the summer of that year, this family of four moved into a brand new house that Dad and his brothers built at 200 Riel Avenue in St. Vital. Bob was born in 1963, and the twins, Denise and Diane, followed four years later.

And so in 1967, Mom was 31 with five kids under 10 years old, and still didn't really know how to cook. "I thought we needed meat, potatoes, and a vegetable. That's pretty much all we ate, but your dad ate anything I made, and didn't complain" said Mom, adding, "that's all I could do with a budget of $40 a week".

And mom had so much more to deal with than budgeting. When the twins came along, they were a full-time job. This left Bob and I to wander the neighbourhood completely unsupervised. Dad used to say that no day could pass without him coming home from work and seeing evidence of this before he got in the door. A broken window, a bent eavestrough, a bicycle lying in the driveway… once he came home to see the garage door completely swabbed with a mop full of mud (Bob, btw). Another time he found me bleeding from the thumb after Bob had thrown a cast iron table saw handle at me. I was immediately found guilty of intimidation, and punished accordingly. All of this happened while mom was coping with raising the twins, meticulously cleaning the house, and ensuring supper was on the table by 5:30 p.m. sharp. It was an impossible task, yet she did it for many years.

A story of note… In 1967, Dad decided that we should go on a family vacation to EXPO in Montreal. In the heat of August, the five of us packed into our 1964 Chevrolet Impala, and pulling a small tent trailer, set off for Quebec. It was very hot, we had no air conditioning, and mom was six months pregnant with twins. Dad was responsible for driving, and setting up the tent trailer. Mom was responsible for the food, and providing three meals a day for the five of us. A highlight of the trip, according to mom, was the one day she was left at the trailer park with three-year-old Bob, while Dad, Bonnie and I went to La Ronde, the EXPO's amusement park.

There are so many stories of mom's selflessness for the benefit of family. We kids certainly didn't make her life easy, but we sure did make it interesting. On behalf of your five kids, 11 grandkids, and at this writing, five great grandkids, all our love and thanks. You were right after all; you weren't a good mom. You were a GREAT mom. THE BEST!

This book would not have been possible without you.

All you need to know about me

Author Robert Fulghum wrote a book called *All I Really Need to Know I Learned in Kindergarten,* which is about living a balanced life, taking naps, and learning to work together. I took kindergarten at the St. Vital United Church, and my teacher was Mrs. Main. I am not sure she taught me all I needed to know; I remember little of that experience beyond playing with coloured plasticine and nap time. I no longer play with plasticine. I counter-postulate the following:

Most of what you need to know about me is indicated in my grade school report cards, which, through some magic and happenstance have followed me through life in an envelope in my memory box.

I'll spare the mundane specifics of grades attained and focus on the comments, which really turned out to be quite insightful, chronologically and one for each year.

Billy is a very good student but sometimes becomes so involved with his friends he forgets to pay attention.
—Miss Unger (Gr. 1)

Billy shows imagination and originality, though he is inclined to be a little lazy with his written work. He is an excellent reader, and always contributes greatly to oral lessons.
—Mrs. Post (Gr. 2)

Bill is a neat and conscientious worker. He puts forth his best effort, is progressing well, and has improved greatly in reading comprehension. When he applies himself, he does excellent work.
—Miss Bartlett (Gr. 3)

Bill's work habits have improved greatly. It's been a pleasure to teach William. Good Luck!
—Mrs. Wright (Gr. 4)

Bill is one of our best math students. He was a bit lazy at the beginning of the year, but caught up to the others as soon as he realized it was important. Bill's achievement puts him near the top of the class. He generally shows good self-control and works well in groups, however, Bill likes to be in a quiet corner when he needs to concentrate on reading. His interest in improvement is spasmodic, but his work is usually satisfactory. He does what is expected of him, and usually on time.
—Mrs. Wilson (Gr. 5)

Reading comprehension very high. Grammar very good. His one weakness is that he doesn't always remember to complete and hand assignments in. Penmanship good. Bill is a "loner", he finds it difficult to concentrate in a group. Bill is often careless about producing neat and complete assignments. I'd like to see him become more conscientious in this respect. Though he continues to neglect his daily work, he achieves surprisingly well on his tests.
—Mrs. Powell (Gr. 6)

In summary then, I guess I seemed bright, but appeared to be lazy and had a short attention span. ADHD might have been suggested, had it been known at the time.

Z is for Zorro!

We didn't have XBox, PlayStation, or even GameCube. We played outdoors, mostly. And we played with what we could find – cardboard boxes, discarded construction materials, whatever. But when we discovered TV's Guy Williams as Zorro, it became our mission to fashion a sword with which we could carve the mark of Zorro (Z) into our enemies, and perhaps, win the hand of the lovely Anna Maria. Not that this was our primary objective. No, that was to have a logical and credible excuse to whip each other with tree branches while screaming *Zorro!*

Surrender, Comandante! Taste my mighty rapier! Each in turn played the part of the greedy, cruel, and slightly inept Captain Enrique Sánchez Monasterio, because, well, there can't be *two* Zorros...

Clearly, we didn't stick too close to the script. And the accuracy of Zorro's signature Z was lost as well; he could slice his mark into a man's shirt without piercing skin, or cut the twine that held up his pants, or both. We would mercilessly try to leave an indelible mark as retribution for one received. Left hand raised and drawn back, we'd advance/parry away until blood was drawn, then answer to our mother's call for supper. The superficial wounds were never revealed.

At least you HAVE GameCube. We used to beat each other with sticks! And we liked it! I said this many times in young fatherhood.

Fast forward to this afternoon, and I am paring down branches of the front yard maple for disposal in the backyard fire pit, when the perfect rapier is unveiled right before my eyes. In a moment I am transported back to 8-year-old me, attempting to out-fence my childhood friend and part-time nemesis, Glenn, who sadly passed away a few years ago of brain cancer. In his honour, I made the classic mark of Zorro in the dirt, and before immolating my weapon, made the classic whipping sound in the air. *En Garde!*

It's in these strange moments I miss my childhood friend. Oh well, gotta go. Time for supper…

And the award goes to...

Summers in the late 60s and early 70s were long and eagerly anticipated. There is no way to accurately express the anticipation of its arrival; not the official date of June 20 or 21, but the actual start of summer one week later at the end of the school year. We burst through the front doors of Minnetonka School, report cards in hand, ready to conquer the world, or at least our little tiny corner of it.

Friday, June 30, 1972 was particularly memorable, as we testosterone-charged preteens emerged from school to the best soundtrack EVER, Alice Cooper's *School's Out*.

That day was probably the best day of my preteen life. I had a good report card, and had just won the school's Citizenship/Sportsmanship Award. Given to a Grade 6 graduate and announced at the school's final assembly to raucous cheering, the award, a large silver cup, was given to the school's best athlete exhibiting signs of good citizenship. The previous winner was Nelson, aka "Smellie", a blonde, curly haired prodigious multi-sport athlete who was admired by all, especially the girls. I'd wanted to be him for an entire year, and purposefully embodied all his best attributes in my Grade 6 year to seal the deal. And I did, through organizing recess baseball/soccer games, competing successfully in the school field day, and regionally at the St. Vital track and field meet. I was inclusive and as fair as possible in selecting teams. I settled disputes. I won and lost with humility and honour. And I did it all for the attention of my buddies, the girls whose attention we wanted, and of course the big silver cup trophy.

The joke was on me however, as all was forgotten over the summer, and this bell-bottomed, long-haired dreamer would have to find another way to distinguish himself.

Minnetonka School

The hallway was long and narrow; concrete block walls separated by a sterile green-tiled floor. Sturdy wooden doors marked Grades 1 through 6, and a small office area where the Principal and his secretary were located. Across the hall the janitor's room, with seating for one, was an eraser-cleaning machine, and boilers to heat the school. Washrooms marked "Boys" and "Girls". It was a perfunctory, utilitarian, soulless box located physically, perhaps metaphorically, across the Red River from the University of Manitoba. It was the concrete manifestation of Alpha and Omega; the latter a dream perhaps out of reach save the frozen ice paths in winter.

Such was Minnetonka School in the 1960s, where hundreds of young minds would be educated and formed. Some 55 years later, a former student's description on an alumni Facebook page dubbed it "a place to be survived". Frankly, it was an academic and cultural outpost at which teachers would begin or end their careers, and where the sons and daughters of blue collar families were schooled in every sense of the word – in bullying, authority, hierarchies, peer pressure, respect, corporal punishment, alliances and allegiances.

In the Minnetonka Elementary School of the 1960s, both friends and enemies were made for life.

While academic studies occurred in the classroom, the playground was where I earned my place among my new friends. Soccer was the game of choice for both summer and winter, though it was actually a hybrid of hockey and soccer. Checking was allowed (mandatory for survival, actually), and so injuries occurred daily. It was "boys only"; an unofficial rule accepted without objection by the girls who watched passively from the sidelines, if they watched at all. We assumed they did, and fought tooth and nail for their attention and admiration. I don't imagine they really cared.

I will always remember my first moment of glory, when I established myself as a contender in the herd. An open free ball some 30 feet away, and the athletic (and older) Gordie and I were on a collision course. We connected shoulder to shoulder at full speed. I threw all of my weight into him, and he went down hard. I kicked the ball downfield, and turned to see him picking himself up, with a look that said "Who the hell are you?" But in that moment, and on that day, many in the school would ask the same question. And I would have six years to provide a more complete answer.

My Winnie Cooper

The Wonder Years was an American coming-of-age TV show that starred Fred Savage as Kevin Arnold, an adolescent boy growing up in a suburban middle class family, set from 1968–1973. When I first saw it I thought *this is my life on television!* I identified with every episode.

Kevin's on-and-off childhood crush on Winnie Cooper provided the tension that kept viewers interested for the show's five-year run. A much older Kevin narrated the show from his adult point of view, with the benefit of life's experience and perspective.

My wife knew where I was going; it was no secret. And as usual, she shrugged it off. *"That's just the way he is."* I was off to meet a childhood crush for another short story, some fifty-plus years after we had first met.

This is not a tale of love at first sight; not really a tale of love at all. I suppose it is more telling of my romantic imaginings, of how a story can write itself in the mind of a creative soul, leaving an indelible imprint without benefit of the substance of fact.

Off in the car I went, to meet her at Tim Hortons. I thought, as I turned into the parking lot, that the story would be so much easier to write if she stood me up. But there she was picking up her coffee; not only on time but just a little bit early. There was no mistaking her, though I suppose I see her through the kindest filters of time, my brain computer filtering out over 50 years of age and experience, distilling down to the angelic face she had at age six when she was introduced to our Grade 1 class as the newest student. And that moment is almost as clear to me today as it was in 1966, when the most beautiful girl I had ever seen – this brown-haired, dimple-cheeked, yellow tam-wearing enigma – would enter my life.

She stood facing the class, with Miss Unger's hand on her shoulder. Behind them, a row of windows to the outside world where, until then, we'd had free reign. In front of them a rag-tag bunch of unruly rurals about to vie for her attention. She was, as it turns out, very shy and a bit nervous. A truly shy person would stare at the ground; she scanned the room managing to avoid eye contact. She would become the girl who everyone wanted to befriend, the centre of an in-group that was not so much of her design as it was organic.

And although she didn't know it, she would become my Winnie. My grade school crush. The girl whose attention I most sought; the one whose smile would light my day, but whose indifference would characterize my childhood. Not that she was my first crush. No, that honour was bestowed a week or so earlier on the Grade 1 teacher, the lovely Miss Unger. They couldn't be more different from each other, and yet they had my infatuation in common. Go figure.

And so here we are some 50-plus years later, reminiscing about growing up in South St. Vital, when we walked the same dirt roads and played in each others' yards, as well as our days at Minnetonka School. She produced a yearbook, but we found ourselves talking about life and kids, and what prompted me to ask for this get-together. I had several distinct memories of her that I wanted to share, with the sole purpose of corroboration so that I could write my story accurately.

We (I mostly) talked about the day we met. About how she liked Juicy Fruit gum, and how I waited for her to ask me for a piece so I could produce a whole pack in response. A memory of a group of us hanging out in the tree fort in her back yard. The time in Joanne's basement where a group of us dared to play spin-the-bottle for the first time, and the game abruptly ended when I spun and the bottle pointed to her. And about how I once drew our initials in the wet cement of Oakridge Bay. The mandatory Valentine card exchanges in school.

And the time she came to my birthday party.

Mom was in the hospital for an operation on my birthday. I was depressed and missed her, so Dad took me to see her. He gave me a tin of butterscotch candy (presumably from the hospital gift shop) as a present. Apparently he was not the birthday shopper in our family. We returned home for what was supposed to be a surprise birthday party, but depressed as hell, I walked past the balloons, streamers and eight or so friends and went straight to my bedroom. I didn't even see them. I was putting the tin on my dresser when I turned to see Cheryl walking towards me, with a big smile. I felt like it was a dream. Others followed in. My mood turned 180 degrees in a moment.

Times like these are burned into my memory, and I have relived them a few times over the years as I related these innocent childhood stories to my kids.

Cheryl and me, 2023

My enthusiasm to verify these stories took a hit however, when, over our Tim Hortons coffees, she shrugged her shoulders and said "I'm sorry, I just don't remember". Initially, I was crestfallen. It was, and is, so vivid in my memory. Hers apparently not so much.

The funny thing is it didn't really matter if she remembered these things, and after all they are MY memories. It mattered that she was there and she had made time for me. And I have a new memory to write about, in case my memory one day fades.

Things never turn out exactly the way you planned. We grow up in a heartbeat. But the memories of childhood, with any luck they remain.

And I still look back, with wonder.

Catch the San at the loop, past the powerlines into the sticks

When I think back to my childhood, the memories play as 8mm Kodachrome film; they are hazy, often out of focus -- snippets randomly stripped together. Edited, perhaps, from their unique imprint in the recesses of my brain. They are, at least, in colour. I wonder if my children, brought up in the age of 4 and 8K imagery, will remember their childhoods in HD. I hope so.

My first conscious memory is of the sound of hammers nailing shingles to the roof of our new home on Riel Avenue in South St. Vital. Three strikes per nail; two if they were on their game. Men carrying heavy bundles of shingles up the wooden ladder, a clap as they were dropped in place, then again, tap, tap, tap. It was a sound repeated often throughout my childhood as urban sprawl took hold in 1960s Winnipeg. To this day I feel hammers play the music of progress.

Riel Avenue was named for the tract of land on which it stands, once owned by the Riel family, whose progeny included the infamous Métis leader and father of Manitoba, Louis Riel. Several hundred feet wide by several kilometres long, their property covered an expanse between the Red River on the west and the Seine River to the east. The Riel home, a few hundred yards from the Red River, has become Riel House, a National Historic Site commemorating Riel's life, and the lives of Métis families in the Red River Settlement. The house is now an island of history in the residential development known as River Pointe, with four rows of upscale houses separating it from its former riverfront status.

In the 1960s, Riel House was a derelict shack on River Road, hidden by an overgrowth of trees and on the verge of collapse, a place for more adventurous kids than I to explore. To its north, a fenced pasture where I fed sweet-smelling clover from the fence line to Queenie, a beautiful honey-coloured horse. To the south, more pasture — that belonging to the McNulty's, who owned idyllic river acreage replete with a two-story log mansion and a true "cement pond" (pool). In between, the St. Vital Hospital. Tucked back into a river bend across from the University of Manitoba, it was a foreboding brown/red brick edifice. Founded as a tuberculosis sanatorium by the Grey Nuns in 1931, it was renamed the St. Vital Hospital in 1961, but it was, to all locals, affectionately nicknamed the "San".

To eight-year-old me, the San was a mystical place; perhaps in my furtive imagination, a house of horrors. Nuns in long brown habits and black veils wielding yardsticks, patrolling the sterile, green-tiled hallways... wardens to children with severe physical and mental disabilities. It was hardly so, but until some of my school friends started volunteering there, that is what I imagined. It was an outpost of where I grew up, and of my imagination. But there was little appreciation in South St. Vital for a boy with an imagination; in fact it was something I might easily be bullied for, and so I kept these thoughts, for the most part, to myself.

Further east was Minnetonka Elementary School; a bleak, utilitarian rectangle divided into six classrooms and sundry office/storage space that smelled of chalk dust and erasers. It is where I acquired my first seven years of education; in academics yes, but also bullying, racism, cliques, fighting, friendship, unimaginable ignorance, and unrequited loyalty. My report cards tell the story of a loner, unwilling to work in groups, who had issues with focus. And yet I still managed to bring home at least one straight A report card, and a citizenship/sportsmanship award of which I was particularly proud. Minnetonka School was three blocks from home, with the sparsely populated avenues of Riverbend, Woodlawn, and Greendell in between.

Coincidentally, I rode my bike down Riel Avenue today with Roula, and in the two blocks approaching our old house recounted short stories for almost every house we passed:

This is where Danny lived. He gave me a baseball as a present. Turned out it belonged to the school. He was a foster child, and didn't show up for school one day. Or ever after.

The Crawfords lived here. Reggie Crawford played in a band in the 60s and they'd practise in that garage.

Those houses there? That's where the Fillion's, Lindsay's, Sired's, and Chorney's lived. That's one of the first few houses on Riel. Doerksen's live there now. Carol is dad's cousin.

I got caught climbing on the roof of that house when it was being built, by Mrs. O'Hara, who lived (me, pointing) in that house. Mrs. Van Bethray lived over there; that's who Bethray Bay was named after. Then there's the Kehler's, Gray's, Neufeld's, and Braun's. And there are four houses where there used to be a big field, where I broke my front tooth while snowmobiling. Then there's Les's house...

I own the fact that my recounting of these things is boring to anyone but those who grew up in the neighbourhood. But when I am there I am transported to a far simpler time. A time of innocence. A time when everyone knew their neighbours – played with them, ate with them, entertained ourselves through harsh winters with them, and generally got along with them. A time when we all shopped at Dakota Village Safeway, and all bought our clothes at the Kmart on Fermor. A time when we all observed Sunday as a day of rest, with no shopping and little activity, save the children playing in the yard.

We stopped at Riel Avenue and Minnetonka Street, the epicentre for all the kids in our neighbourhood, where still stands the hydro pole that was ground zero for our favourite game of Ghost Ghost, our version of Hide and Seek. When it came on, the streetlight atop the pole signaled time for bed. I touched the pole.

"This," I explained to Roula, *"was home."*

What'd you get?

Alpine 6–3234...

"Hello?"
"Hi. Is Glenn there?"
"Merry Christmas Billy!"
"Uh, Merry Christmas Auntie Flo. Is Glenn there?"
"GLE-ENNN! PHONE!"

Christmas morning followed the same pattern for many years. Glenn would occasionally make the call, but more often I would call first, anxious to find out what he got for Christmas. Then with permission, we'd trot across the street to check out each other's haul.

Glenn was my best friend; two years my senior, and though not an only child, he wasn't one of five. The resulting math gave him a distinct advantage in the early years. I recall his Christmas presents more than my own; Strombecker race car set, Meccano erector set, ping pong table... he had the knack of making me feel like my presents didn't measure up. It didn't really matter; most of our toys required at least two to play. But it was a competition, and though we were happy for each other there was pride in winning the day.

The 1960s Peters family Christmases were officially underway with the Bethel Mennonite Christmas Eve church service. Opened with cringeworthy piano solos by kids whose feet dangled above the pedals, through to the teenage prodigies (I particularly remember the Kroeker boys); participants equally elicited the pride of their respective parents. Then carol singing in both official languages of the Mennonites, English and German, the latter sung phonetically (by the youth, anyway) from the words printed in the hymnal. Though it took years to master the proper pronunciation, I never did understand much of what I was singing...

Stille Nacht, heilige Nacht,
Alles schläft; einsam wacht...

Back then, loudly singing "highly gay nacht" might have been met with suspicion; rather the opposite from the elders who assumed we were swept up in the moment (still makes me snicker). The sermon that followed was rendered insufferably long by the one-liner in the program: *Goodie bags will be distributed immediately after the service for those aged 12 and under.* Candy canes, leftover Halloween caramels, licorice and assorted hard candy, weighted with a real Mandarin orange... I have such fond memories of trading with Bonnie and Bob in the cold back seat of the car on the ride home.

We opened our gifts on arrival, or at least after mom got out some desserts and made coffee. Then we'd take our places near the Christmas tree. Never the best one on the lot (or even *from* a lot), and certainly not a Douglas Fir, but a hand-cut, volume underestimated, bad-side-to-the-wall, Charlie Brown Christmas tree. Lovingly decorated with cards, popcorn strings, and school-made red/green paper chains, frosted with spray snow, finished with tinsel, and topped with a lighted plastic angel, it was transformed into the best tree ever. The tinsel was later discontinued when we found a strand protruding from the cat's rear end.

My parents always kept one present back so that we'd have something from "Santa" to open Christmas morning. Whoever woke up first would wake the others, and then knock on mom and dad's bedroom door to ask if we could open our "big gifts". Then we'd scramble to the living room to see what had been placed there, mysteriously, over night. Once again, Mom would test the little patience we had by making coffee. After we tore open our gifts, Dad always asked if we'd had a good Christmas. I don't think I ever really appreciated how much an enthusiastic "Yes!" meant to him. There were banner years (1973, brand new set of blue sparkle Coronet drums) and bleak years (late 60s, used puzzles with missing pieces) and the usual clothes, pyjamas, and socks. Toblerones and assorted nuts in the Christmas stockings. And the stuff I miss most... hugs from Auntie Kay, family laughter, playing Rumoli on the kitchen table, even the annual box of Pot of Gold chocolates received from Uncle Isaac.

Shortly after a quick breakfast, we'd be off to Grandma Peters' house in Plum Coulee, where some of my aunts, uncles, and cousins would gather. As I recall, we were not allowed to bring our new toys to play with, so the cousins would just hang out until faspa (cold meats, bread, cheese and pickles) was served, listening to Dad and the uncles argue (they always argued) while Mom and the aunts would assist Grandma in the kitchen. After faspa, we entertained ourselves by exploring Grandma's closets (still full of our deceased Grandpa's clothes), the attic, and the basement replete with cistern, scary early 1900s pictures of long-dead relatives, and dusty preserves. I loved my Grandmother dearly, but when it was time to leave we were more than ready to go. But not home...

The next stop was Auntie Kay's house for Christmas dinner. In stark contrast to the Peters uncles, visits to Auntie Kay's were laid back and fun. Time with Grandpa Robb, who died when I was 13, was precious. After he passed away the tradition moved to our house. A turkey dinner with all the trimmings – cranberry sauce, turnips, mashed potatoes with gravy, pierogies with fried onions and sour cream, cabbage rolls, tomato jelly from a fish mould, ... all on a beautifully decorated table, with a glass of tomato juice and a party "cracker" at each Johnson Brothers "The Friendly Village" china setting. How I took those times for granted. To this day I think of those who have passed, whose loving presence or loud Low German arguments, then tolerated, are now treasured memories.

My family all knows I am a big fan of the television series *The Curse of Oak Island*, where, despite millions of dollars in excavating equipment, the best finds have been unearthed by metal detection expert Gary Drayton. And so I was particularly excited one recent Christmas morning to receive a metal detector! Like my dad, Roula looked right at me to gauge my happiness. It was very thoughtful; perfect, in fact. Once again we'd had a wonderful Christmas, blessed with family, food, and fellowship.

I just wish I could have called Glenn to ask *"What'd you get?"*, but in 2016 he passed into memory along with my dad, Auntie Kay, Grandpa Robb, Grandma Peters, and many of the aunts and uncles. God Bless their memories, especially at Christmas.

Those summer days

Some songs bring me back to a time and place in my life. Sly and the Family Stone's *Hot Fun in the Summertime* is one of those, and the time was the late evening of August 22, 1969. The first few notes always transport me to our home's front steps on that humid and record hot thirty-six degree summer night, straining to see what the neighbours were up to across the street at the post wedding reception party. The impossibly handsome Brian Kelly had swept away the equally impossibly beautiful Sandra Wiens, on whom I'd had a childhood crush for years; she being my favourite of several neighbourhood babysitters. Some 60 family members and neighbours filled their home to overflowing, from the basement bar to the garage. Everyone that I could see had a drink in their hand, and it was loud. Very loud.

Despite the happy lyrics of the song, it has come to be a signpost of my life; signifying the sad but inevitable march into puberty. I would be over Sandra in a week, focusing my puppy love upon another, then another...

Earlier that evening our family had attended the reception in the basement of the Dakota Hotel. Dressed in my Sunday best, I wandered aimlessly among the guests, looking for anyone my age to talk to. No luck. It was, I believe, the first wedding reception I'd ever attended. It was loud, and full of friendly handshaking, back-slapping and banter. The neighbours were all there, though it was strange to see them all dressed up, with drinks in hand (alcohol!), laughing and smiling and... lining up?

I had no idea what was going on, but I knew I wanted to be a part of it. I tucked into the line and glanced ahead. Food maybe? Drinks? I would duck out if that were the case. At nine years old definitely too young for that, and being Mennonite, well, that was strictly verboten. Turned out it was actually a receiving line. I moved through the elder family members, was enthusiastically greeted by Mr. Wiens, and then I found myself face-to-face with Leona, Maid of Honour and sister of the bride, who did not hesitate to plant a kiss on my cheek. I was stunned. I don't think I'd ever been kissed before. I was speechless, and with the sudden influx of blood to my cheeks, perhaps a little bit dizzy. It was all happening so fast...

Sandra, certainly the most beautiful bride I'd ever seen, was next. She took her cue from Leona and planted a kiss on me. Could have been on my cheek, maybe my lips, I nearly blacked out so I can't remember. Then I shook Brian's hand, nodded at his familial entourage, and found my way to a chair. What had just happened? Why was my heart racing? What did I think of all this? If I remember one thing clearly from that evening more than 50 years later, is that I recovered, rejoined the line, and got two more kisses. And more than one confused look.

The party across the street would stretch well into the night, and as my parents were there, the five of us kids went unsupervised. With the living room stereo playing the hits of the summer of 1969, I sat on the steps and imagined the fun the adults must be having at the send-off party for Sandra and Brian.

But mostly I reflected on the kisses. Oh, those summer days!

The dog catcher

He was short by today's standards, maybe five foot two, with plenty of distinguishing characteristics – a military-style brush cut, furrowed Jimmy Cagney brow with the whiny, high-pitched voice to match, that immediately cut through (barked over actually) a cacophony of elementary school kids. He'd cruise the schools of South St. Vital; the brown, square van with cargo doors at the back, like the paddy wagons used to take prisoners to Headingly jail. He'd slow to a crawl by the bike racks at the front of the school. Then stop, stare, and scribble into his notepad. He appeared ex-military; perhaps not front line due to his size; maybe a mess tent prep cook. His brown uniform, replete with service cap, gave him an aura of authority. There'd be murmurs on the playground, worse still, rumours that he'd used handcuffs one time. He terrified us all. Or at least those of us with a dog, or a bike.

He was the City of St. Vital Dog Catcher.

In the mid-60s, everyone I knew had a dog. In my neighbourhood alone, Taylors had Wolf, the Wiens had Omen, Lewers had Bart, MacRaes had Haemish… and we had Penny, a Golden Retriever. And there were no fenced yards. Some had kennels (in Wolf's case, a car chain and a stake in the ground kept him at bay), but most dogs had the run of the neighbourhood. Kids those days learned to respect their space, and bites were rare. And if you came home with a bite hole in your jeans you'd likely be asked what you did to provoke the dog! Of course free-range dogs had their pros and cons, the latter being the sight/smell of poop slowly emerging in the melting snow come springtime. Cleanup was my annual misfortune.

Penny's dog tags

Bicycle licensing predates the 1960s, but there seemed to be a renewed effort put forward by the City to enforce mandatory licensing. Public service announcements on TV. Notes sent home from school. All of my friends thought they were cool looking, and made us feel "grown up" to pilot a licensed vehicle. However, despite the City's urging most of us were simply advised by our parents to leave our bikes at home if we didn't want to lose them. The ball was firmly in our court, and as the Dog Catcher was given the added responsibility of enforcement, he became our de facto arch enemy.

WILLIAM J PETERS

And so our army of skinny kids glared back. We imagined an uprising; flanking right and left, distracting from the front while opening the back doors to set the prisoners free. Someone would "pants" him if he dared get out of the truck, maybe stick a potato in the tailpipe for good measure. Then off to school as conquering heroes... but we did none of these things. We did learn that if you lock your bikes together, and to the rack, your chances of losing your bike went down dramatically. Or at least that was our response.

I don't know of anyone who lost a dog or bike to this man, but I do know that we were terrified at that prospect. And maybe that was the point.

The devaluation of Coke

We have a refrigerator/freezer in the kitchen, as most people do. It's bigger than the one we had growing up, probably by four cubic feet. In the old days one was standard; there might be a beer fridge in the rec room, but that was Dad's territory and perusing the contents was *verboten*. Of course we had a deep freeze containing the standard fare of the 1960s... ground beef, a roast or two, a few loaves of white bread, a few small pickerel, perhaps some deer steaks if Dad had been successful that Fall. And ice, which we would add to the Coleman cooler to keep the sandwiches fresh for Sunday picnics in the park. If we were lucky, there would be Kool-Aid, and luckier still if it was grape!

Conversely, our present-day basement has a room dedicated to food storage, with a seven-foot tall pantry cabinet for the dry goods and canned items, an eighteen cubic foot refrigerator/freezer, and a twenty-two cubic foot vertical freezer. No deer parts or white bread therein, just a myriad of prepared foods that can be heated up with little notice. Foods representing countries like China (spring rolls), Greece (phyllo pastry) Ukraine (pierogies... ok I'm pushing it here), Canada (Atlantic cod) and some South American nations (coffee). It's remarkable, really, that we lived through the 1960s without this stuff.

However, the centre of new-age decadence in our food storage facility is the fridge. As I write this, there are at least two cases of pop, a jug or two of orange juice, assorted cheeses, and bottles of Perrier, wine, and margarita mix. There's also a Costco-sized jar of pickle juice. No pickles, just the juice. I have no idea.

We were a family of seven in the late 60s, and food was more utilitarian in those days. Our Scottish mother was not the cook in her family, that being the purvey of Auntie Kay, who shooed her younger sister out of the house when meals were being prepared. And so, by her own admission, her knowledge of food prep was limited to meat, potatoes, and a vegetable. The vegetable was often canned peas, a putrid green slop that was "cheap and easy" (I am directly quoting my mom here). As we were told to clear our plates before leaving the table – upon penalty of death – I saved it for last, nodded thanks to Mom, and made a beeline for the washroom. Under the pretext and cover of washing my hands, I'd spit them down the toilet.

Summer barbecues were a treat, especially if someone other than my dad was at the grill (rarely the case). We'd line up Oliver Twist style, buns held outstretched with anticipation, until dad deposited a lump of coal camouflaged with bbq sauce. Like Krampus at Christmas. It did not grow hair on my chest either! I was 23 before I ate a properly prepared steak. It was other-worldly. I've been a medium-rare man ever since.

My wife is an excellent cook, always trying new things with amazing results. This is not reflected in the contents of our freezer. That is the influence of Christian, who has his supper when the spirit moves and demands of him that he eat it from the microwave. In true Greek tradition, his wish is his mother's Costco bill. As it is written, so shall it be done!

My brother Bob and I used to accompany our dad on tree jobs, dad's way of hard-earning the money he used to keep food on the table. We were responsible to collect the logs and branches as they fell, and pack them into the back of the 1949 Mercury. It was hard work. I remember on one particularly hot day we were removing a tree in River Heights. We had started mid-morning and were working well into the afternoon when the woman of the house came out to watch. Dad stopped the chainsaw and came down from the tree to talk to her; clients often saved payment until the work was at least halfway done. We kept working; hoping to catch up enough to take a break. I vividly recall her asking if "the boys would like a 7-Up or Coke". It wouldn't have been unusual for him to decline on our behalf, but in this case we were allowed to accept.

It was heaven. Today there is no equivalent.

Which brings me back to our basement refrigerator, and 2021. I noticed we're out of Coke, and low on Pepsi and Canada Dry ginger ale. I hope Christian hasn't noticed.

Dropmore memories

Several times in the late 1960s, our family of seven would spend the weekend near my mother's hometown of Dropmore, 400 kilometres north-west of Winnipeg. Specifically, at the farm of Phil and Barb Zimmer, close friends of Mom's family for many years. We literally filled their home; took over, in fact, all of the spare bedrooms and couches. We kids called them auntie and uncle, and they fussed over us like we were their own.

Memories still invoke all the olfaction that a farm with pigs, chickens and cattle can. The fetid smell of the pig pen. The fusty and dilapidated barn that we were told never to enter for fear of collapse. The rank chicken coop, and the pungency of fresh cow pie. Of course you become noseblind once you get used to it, and so we were able to fully enjoy the good smells (and tastes) as well… the fresh baking, garden strawberries or raspberries served with fresh cream; milk sometimes served with a playful squirt direct from the cow, courtesy uncle Phil. Bonnie and I vied for the bed with the softest mattress (broken springs, truth be told), and whoever won would invariably sleep in. Bacon, eggs, pancakes and toast in the morning; orange juice for the kids, strong coffee for the adults. Then out to play with the dog and cats in the glorious petrichor of this farm paradise, and perhaps search for sun-bleached bones in the surrounding forest. Armed with my Crosman pellet gun – to protect us from the wolves and bears, of course!

For us city kids, it was an incredible and earthy otherworld which we imagined we were the first to explore.

In 1993 Roula and I passed through Dropmore on a somewhat circuitous route to Vancouver Island. I wanted to share my memories with her, including the time I spent in the town where my mother grew up, and where my Grandfather managed the grain elevator... but it, and the rail tracks leading to it, was gone. I stood in a field waving my hands about in description of what had been. My patient wife stood and watched. And so, frustrated (well, me; Roula was understandably confused), we proceeded to the Zimmer farm a few kilometres down the highway. Thank God the farm was still there, but the barn was gone, and much of the forest had been graded into piles to make way for grain fields. I knocked on the door I once flew through. Nobody was home. Barb and Phil had, only months earlier, retired to nearby Russell.

Phil and Barb seemed old, even before then. But some 35 years later, Barb managed to come in to the city to help my parents celebrate their 50th wedding anniversary.

Undeterred by even more passage of time, the other day I drove the 400 plus kilometres to Dropmore, and relived the 1993 experience with Christian. He was similarly unimpressed with the town. If only he could see what, in my mind's eye, I saw...

Some 50 years prior I had, against orders, left the farm to walk in sweltering heat, the two miles into town. Now retracing the route in reverse, I wanted to show Christian just how daring this trip had been. We'd find the farm, and perhaps knock on the door again. And then the stories would flood back with which I'd regale him to pass the time on the journey home. But the farm, with all its outbuildings, even the surrounding forest in which we hunted for petrified animal skeletons, was gone. In its place a field of canola stretched into the horizon. If that field could talk.

Now all that was, exists in memory only. How fleeting life is.

There's no place like home

My earliest recollection of my paternal grandparents centered around their farm, located a mile and a half north of Plum Coulee. We rarely visited without the accompaniment of family; generations of aunts, uncles and cousins. There was always food and conversation (mostly Low German), and it was an important time of connecting. Those times dwindled in quantity and quality when they moved off the farm and into town. And a few years after the untimely death of Grandpa Peters, Grandma moved to Maple Grove Manor, then Salem Home in Winkler, where she died in 1997.

I was born February 9, 1960 at the Women's Pavilion in Winnipeg, Canada, to Bill and Irene Peters of 948 Riviera Crescent in the suburb of Fort Garry. They would bring me home a few days later.

It was the first place I lived, but I have no recollection of time spent there.

With my arrival came the reality that the family, numbering four, had outgrown the tiny riverbank property and would have to move. Dad and his brother-in-law Harry built 224 Riel Avenue in the summer of 1960 across the river in St. Vital, and my sister Bonnie and I would have a brand new house in which to live. The most memorable moments of our childhood were spent there; our family expanded by one with the arrival of my brother Bob in 1963, and again by two with my twin sisters, Diane and Denise, in 1967. I attended elementary, junior high and high school, all while living there, until 1979 when I moved to Steinbach to work.

Over the next few years I would live in East Kildonan (a few months), St. Vital (a year or so), then back with my parents while I went to College (two years). Then off to Winkler, MB for two years, back to

Fort Richmond for a few months, finally settling in at 772 Centennial in River Heights, where I lived when I met and married Roula. We lived there until our family split the seams of that house with the arrival of Olivia in 1994 and Christian in 1997. In the summer of 1997 we moved to our current family home.

Agnes "Grandma" Peters

Current events and conversation have given me pause to consider the meaning of home. Certainly I have spent time living in different houses, some for more than a few years, some for a few months. Riel Avenue was home, so too was Minnetonka Street, Centennial

Avenue and where we live now. And simply, the answer is found in being surrounded by family. *Home is where your heart is*, as they say.

Riviera Crescent wasn't home, to me at least. I lived there, but with no recollection of the time it just doesn't seem to qualify. With many sad/happy memories, Riel definitely qualifies as home. Centennial was where Roula and I started our family, and though it was home for a time, it seems now to have been a transitional place. Our current home was where we *really* started to make memories; it is the definition of home for us now and for the foreseeable future.

So it would seem that one makes a house into a home, through filling it with lasting memories of family and friends. I'm good with that.

In her final years, Grandma Peters often told stories about home, which in her case meant either the Peters farm, or the Wiens farm of her early childhood. However, on one of my last visits to see her at Salem Home, and in one of her most thoughtful and salient moments, she told me where she would most like to be. Not with her family on the Wiens farm, or in her beloved garden at the Peters farm, both of which were full of beautiful memories. She looked at me with her beautiful blue eyes, and I knew exactly what she would say. What many say in the last days and hours of their life.

She simply looked up and said *"I want to go home."*

One small step for man, one giant break for Dropmore squirrel

On July 20, 1969, the Apollo 11 space mission landed the first two people on the Moon – Commander Neil Armstrong and lunar module pilot Buzz Aldrin. The landing brought to fruition President John F. Kennedy's commitment on May 25, 1961 to further space exploration by landing men on the moon within the decade:

"I believe that this nation should commit itself to achieving the goal, before this decade is out, of landing a man on the moon and returning him safely to the Earth."

It was an amazing time to be alive; the event was arguably the most dramatic and important of the 20th century. The equally groundbreaking TV broadcast was watched, worldwide, by an estimated 600 million people. Time stood still on that day.

And nowhere on earth was that more apparent than in my mother's hometown of Dropmore, Manitoba (pop. 60, give or take). For on that day, in the midst of a two-week "holiday", nine-year-old Billy Peters came in from the dry prairie heat to watch the only thing on CBC-TV.

The Barnett's were a lovely old couple, retired and residing in the town. They'd been to Winnipeg to visit friends, and I don't think they expected to be returning with me, but there we were. My reluctance to go gave in to the promise of a six-hour train ride (my first), and that I could take my trusty Czech-made Slavia pellet gun along and shoot to my heart's content.

And so I did, but after a few days ran out of pellets and things to shoot at. And the days are long in Dropmore, very long. And although I am sure the Barnett's tried, there would have been more than a country mile between my idea of fun and theirs. Within a week I would be on my way home, by Grey Goose bus lines this time.

But on that fateful day, in the evening of Sunday the 20th of July, 1969, while Armstrong and Aldrin were safely back in the lunar module, I wrote my first ever letter to home:

Dropmore, Man.
July 20, 1969

Dear Mom, Dad + Family,
I had a very good time on the train. I learned that if you press a button on the seat and push back on the seat the seat bends back and then you have a bed. I am having a good time in Dropmore. My shooting has improved a lot. I shot a squirrel with my gun three times and never killed it. They are building a new road along Uncle Phil's place. I am going to give Bonnie a gopher tail and Bob some samples of rock.
Good-bye for now,
Billy

"That's one small step for man, one giant leap for mankind."

Yeah, whatever. I am not sure what indicated that my shooting skills had improved, but the most important event of the 20th century, for that squirrel at least, were three missed shots.

Mandingo!

The Pembina Drive-In Theatre opened July 19, 1949. Built by Jack Miles, it was the first drive-in theatre in the Canadian mid-west. The Miles family at one time owned and operated 18 movie theatres in Winnipeg, including The Uptown, The Palace, The Plaza, The Rose and The Roxy theatres. Jack Miles died in 1951.

I was born nine years later, in February of 1960, and for the first months of life lived on a tiny riverfront property at 948 Riviera Crescent. From our back yard, a panoramic view of the Red River and St. Vital Park to the east, and to the south the yet-to-be-developed communities of University Heights and Fort Richmond.

In the summer of 1960 our family moved to Riel Avenue, in the relative wilds of South St. Vital. Riel would eventually extend to River Road, which runs along the Red River toward St. Vital Park. But for most of the 1960s and early 70s my boundaries ended with Riel Avenue and it wasn't until our neighbourhood started to expand that I found my way on my bike through bush trail and dirt road to River Road and St. Vital Park... and an unobstructed closer view of the Pembina Drive-In Theatre.

It was a glorious time for adventure, as developers provided us boys with sand and clay hills to climb, from basement dugouts. Sounds of drilling, sawing and hammering filled the air each day, and at night an infinite playground awaited. And it wasn't too long before word spread that, if you found your way to River Road just past dark, you could see the "R" movies playing across the river at the Pembina.

One of the hits of the previous summer (1974), *Dirty Mary, Crazy Larry* had what every 14-year-old boy needed: fast cars, women, and sex. It starred Peter Fonda (*Easy Rider*), and a halter-topped actress by the name of Susan George. "There's nothin' they won't try!" promised the film, which included (spoiler alert) trying to beat a train to a crossing at the end. There would be no Dirty Mary, Crazy Larry II.

There would, however, be another Susan George movie the following summer, the R-rated and thus off-limits *Mandingo*. And it was drawing boys like flies to the east bank of the Red River in the summer of 1975.

The movie was set on a plantation in the Deep South of the United States prior to the American Civil War.

Boxer Ken Norton would play a prize-fighting Mandingo slave.

Susan George would play Blanche, a social climber and sexually promiscuous daughter of the plantation owner.

And that's all an adventurous 15-year-old boy would need to know.

Of course we all exchanged knowing glances at school when the topic came up, but the truth was most of us had to be home at sunset, scenes with nudity would likely come well into the film, and none of us had the will to fight the mosquitoes into the night anyway.

Bush party busted

Looking back, I'm amazed at the nerve we had. David's parents were away for the weekend, and he had the keys, so off we went in his dad's truck to a bush party by the perimeter. Oh, to be 15 again!

Bush parties happened almost every weekend in what is now Duff Roblin Provincial Park, though I had never been to a big one until this particular Friday. It was exciting to drive there, as we were both 15 and had no business driving unlicensed. I would never have had the nerve to take my dad's truck, but I was fine with being a passenger in this... adventure. We were both experienced drivers, having driven for a few years on the farm by then. Dave drove cautiously, staying just under the posted speed limit. Once parked, we waded into the wooded area by the river into a secluded spot. There must have been 30 people there, most by the bonfire but couples could be seen (and heard) in the bushes nearby. I guess that's how 15-year-old kids got their privacy in those days. Not my scene, but whatever. I attended quite a few parties back in the day as an observer. My elementary school report card did indicate I was a loner of sorts...

Inevitably the beer supply got low, and Dave was asked to make a "beer run" to the nearby St. Norbert Hotel. We hadn't brought any beer, but the fringe benefit of doing the beer run was free beer for the evening, so off we went; Dave, Gord, and me. Gord must have had ID; he was the same age as us, and he might have thought he looked 18, though none of us did, really.

Dave expertly navigated the narrow trail to Courchaine Road, then over the Floodway bridge, all the while planning who would do what at the hotel. I'd never been to a vendor and Dave looked his age, so Gord would handle the transaction. Dave had collected the money, so he would hand it over when we got there. That left me as the...

lookout? I believe we were still discussing our plan as Dave rolled through the stop sign at Turnbull Drive.

Then came the flashing red and blue lights.

You can tell a lot about a person by how they react in a stressful situation. Dave quickly analyzed options. There were none. I stayed put, immediately resigned to accept the consequences. Hey, I was just a passive participant, right? Gord tried to climb over me and jump out the door. "We haven't done anything wrong!" I said. Gord persisted, but my quick reasoning won the moment. "They have guns, Gord." The RCMP, lights flashing, followed us to a stop.

While they ran the licence plate, Gord continued to put forward his argument. They wouldn't shoot, would they? Does the RCMP use tracking dogs?

"Licence and reg..." The officer stopped. Our innocent faces gave us away immediately. "Ok boys, out of the truck." We complied.

I wish I had a picture of that moment. The three of us, side by side, standing spread-eagled with our faces pressed against the truck. The officers made the most of their time, warning of theft charges, driving unlicensed and underage, and anything else they could think of, and Gord and I were perfectly willing to throw Dave under the bus if it meant walking away.

"Ok boys, get in the car. We're taking you home."

I was still optimistic there'd be no consequences; they'd drop us off at the sidewalk and we'd wave goodbye. Hopefully they'd turn the flashers off so the neighbours wouldn't notice. The ride was pretty cool actually, part of me wanted to be seen. Yeah, they caught us this time...

Gord's house was the first stop, and we didn't get to wave goodbye. The officer walked him to the door and rang the bell. I couldn't see his dad's face, but from Gord's I could see it wasn't going well. The officer shook Mr. H's hand and the door closed. The porch light turned off before he got back to the car.

I instinctively reached for the doorknob when we walked up to the back door. The officer pushed my hand down. "Ring the bell."

This persona non grata status was new to me; startling and upsetting. I'd swung through that door thousands of times, and never needed permission. To stand there and wait was, in itself, humiliating. All I could hope for in this moment was for my mom to answer the door.

The door opened wide enough for me to see that my parents were entertaining a couple from church in the basement. Wonderful. Mom peered up from the bottom of the stairs. Dad was standing in front of me, though I continued to look past him at mom.

"Mr. Peters? We pulled your son and his friends over this evening for running a stop sign. He was a passenger in the vehicle, which we believe was taken without permission. As none of the boys have their driver's licence, we are taking them home. Do you have any questions?"

Dad paused and squinted at the officer in the dim porch light. I thought he was considering asking the officer to lock me up. In fact, I was sure of it. I was going to pay dearly for embarrassing him in front of, of all people, church friends!

Instead he smiled.

"Hey Bruce. How've you been?"

"Bill! I thought I recognized you. Good, thanks."

I slipped through the door as they continued talking. Dad never asked for any details, then or after. I have often wondered if he'd done worse in his teens. I never asked.

The goal

It seemed that Dad was always working.

When I look back I wish he'd spent more time with me. Don't get me wrong, we spent lots of time together; mowing the lawn, weeding the garden, cutting trees... when I was a kid there was just no time for hanging out. But that's what I enjoyed most. Just sitting on the couch, watching TV. It didn't happen often, but when it did, it might be on a Saturday night, watching *Hockey Night in Canada*. Anybody versus Jean Béliveau and the Montreal Canadiens. After the game I'd go out on the street and shoot a puck between two blocks of snow. He scores! In those moments, I WAS Jean Béliveau... scoring the winning goal with Dad proudly applauding from the stands.

My actual entry into the hockey world at age 12 was not that easy. Money was tight in those days, and equipment was expensive. I was over the moon with excitement when Dad relented, and told me to get in the car; I was going to play community club hockey, and we were going for skates!

Off we went in the early evening darkness of winter, not to Athlete's Wear or Baldy Northcott's, not Canadian Tire or even Kmart. I don't know that it mattered to me where we went, I was getting a new pair of skates! But when the door of the tiny Norberry Shoe Repair shop opened, the earthy smell of leather and gassy shoe polish filled my lungs and lessened my expectations. There were no new skates here, just a rack of well-used repaired ones, and not many at that. I was in luck; the shopkeeper in the weathered leather apron eyed me up and down and recommended a sharp looking pair of size eights. Dad overruled, and a few minutes and dollars later we left with a beat up pair of size nines. "You can wear two pairs of socks until you grow into them." Fifty years later, I still blame my pronated ankle on those skates.

I thought my luck had changed when Dad told me to go to the Tétrault's house to collect the rest of my gear. André, two years my senior, had a complete set of pads and matching sweater/socks for me! I raced there after dinner, full of youthful expectations and hope. I left with utilitarian shoulder pads that dated back to the 1940s, shin pads three inches too short, tourniquet-tight elbow pads so small they imprinted my skin, pants – not with the requisite suspenders, but belted with a shoelace. (Not that I needed the shoelace, as I had to squeeze them on like a girdle.) They too were three inches short, exposing the garter connections to the threadbare socks, which matched the Montreal Canadiens sweater (in that it too was threadbare and several sizes too small).

"There!" said André. I looked like a cast reject from *Les Misérables*. Or with my exposed garter, maybe *Cabaret*...

Greendell Community Club's Peewee B hockey Coach Hourd took one look at me while I pulled the ragged sweater over my WWII shoulder pads. He rolled his eyes while Coach Chorley more subtly said "Those look, uh, sturdy." The other kids were stunned.

Of course all of this would be moot once I showed them the deft stickhandling moves I'd practised to perfection on the street in front of my house, but it's a new game altogether when oversized skates replace winter boots. And I could barely skate. Backwards? No sir. Hourd and Chorley would have their work cut out for them.

I persevered. I practised. In fact in one season I progressed so much I occasionally played on the first line! (Only after Coach Hourd advised Dad that I needed skates that fit properly, according to Mom.)

I clearly recall a goal I scored that year (ok, maybe the only goal) in a tournament at St. Vital Arena. It was a Saturday morning; the sun shone brightly through the south-facing arena windows. A left winger, I blocked a point shot with my now oversized shin pad upgrades.

Skating past the defence, I had 100 feet of ice to cover before taking my shot, and I was flying as fast as my skinny legs would take me. A famous sportswriter once described a Rocket Richard goal, "... with the flick of a wrist and the bulge of the twine"... it was something like that. I do not remember that part. I do remember that with great speed comes... the boards. I crashed into them full force. But I didn't care – in that moment I was, once again, Jean Béliveau! We celebrated that goal all the way back to the bench, and later in the dressing room, even though we lost. I finally felt like I was part of a team. And in the following edition of the *Lance* community newspaper, submitted, I was told recently, by my mom:

The Peewee B team lost by a close 2–1 score on Saturday. However, the whole team played a fine game and really put all their effort into it. Bill Peters scored the only goal. Nice going, Bill!

I lived for that moment, and assumed all of St. Vital read that report. My efforts were further and unexpectedly rewarded when Dad paid for a team jacket, made to match the others my teammates got the year before. Exactly the same, except for one detail – they spelled Greendell Green*dale*. It was the same, but not quite. That would be thematic of the rest of my hockey playing days.

If Dad was proud of me for scoring that goal, I don't remember. He tended to look beyond the moment, and if he was, he wouldn't have told me anyway. And as I found out in later years, he wasn't even a hockey fan – his sport was baseball. Years later he explained that he thought hockey was too violent. He just liked the gentlemanly way Béliveau played.

Looking back now, I realize why the validation of the *Lance*, however biased and artificial, meant everything to me.

Breaking the ice

It wasn't unusual in the 70s for a group of kids to walk a mile or two in subzero temperatures to go skating or tobogganing, so when a few of us got "Snurfers" for Christmas, off we went.

Usually St. Vital Park would be the destination of choice. Safely located on our side of the river, it was about a 30-minute walk from the neighbourhood. The hill of choice was next to the toboggan slides, and would have zero powder to test the edges of our boards. Someone suggested we cross the river and try the hill on the west side, behind one of the apartment blocks. None of us had ever crossed the river at that point in our lives. We looked at each other. Had any of us been told, specifically, NOT to cross the river? No! So off we went.

The Snurfer board was a predecessor to the modern snowboard, only it had raised staples instead of bindings, and a rope from the tip that you held on to for "stability". It found more function as a means to drag the board up the hill.

I spent at least as much time on my butt as I spent snurfing. The hill was well used by our neighbours from Fort Garry, and had become icy and rock hard. Not quite the powdered slopes of the flashy commercials we'd seen. It didn't take long before the falls and -20° temperature had us call it a day. And so we headed home.

I'd like to say my judgement was affected by the falls, or perhaps the cold, but when I saw the sign stuck in the river ice I had to get a closer look.

CAUTION – THIN ICE

My friends had already moved along the riverbank, about 50 feet away. Then they stopped and watched as I tested the veracity of the City of Winnipeg signage.

"Don't!" warned the elders. But they weren't close enough to assess the ice thickness. I took a step. "Don't!" They repeated emphatically. I had their full attention now. Another step. Then a cracking sound.

I could have retraced my steps, but for reasons only a 12-year-old in the 1970s could understand, I doubled down. "It's not that bad!" I yelled, and to demonstrate, I jumped up, and straight down… through the ice.

My friends, all of them, watched in horror while I went down. Not slowly and dramatically, but as sudden as a magician's trick. Now you see me, now you don't. In a flash and with a splash. I didn't have warning or time to react. I just broke through the ice (yes, it was thin!) and felt the shock of the icy river water over my legs, and then my chest. And then, just as suddenly as I broke through, the falling sensation stopped and I felt a sharp pain in my armpit.

The Snurfer, which I had tucked under my arm for the journey home, had stopped the descent.

My friends, still frozen in their tracks, had a decision to make. And in a moment I knew that they decided that THEY were in trouble. And they would not compound the trouble they were in by coming to my aid. "Hurry up!" they called. This was not bad advice, as the water began to freeze my legs and constrict my breathing. So I kicked my legs furiously, and used the board to scrape my way out of the watery hole, inch by inch, to safety.

I don't remember talking to anyone as we walked the mile home, but I am certain that we agreed it would be in our collective interest to keep the story to ourselves. Now, to quietly get through the back door and…

"Where have you been?" asked Mom. "Get those jeans off, they're soaked!" she added.

She never asked why, and I did not volunteer any details. I climbed out of my frozen pants, stood them up on the landing, and then carefully bent them in half to thaw in the laundry room...

I told this story to my mom recently. She shrugged. "I had your brother and the twins to worry about," she said. "You came home and you were alive. That's all I needed to know."

Robert Marvin "Bobby" Hull

A quick visit with Dr. Swartz in his Boyd Building clinic and I was free to explore downtown for the rest of the afternoon. At 13, that freedom rarely presented itself.

I usually bought my records at Music City, but on that day I decided to check out Autumn Stone, a decidedly more "hip" record shop. With no money for an album on that day, I left empty-handed. Then a well-dressed man in his mid thirties approached, purposefully. He was about the same height as me, but powerfully built. "Excuse me, but do you know where I can find Hanford Drewitt?" he asked.

And that's the first time I met Robert Marvin "Bobby" Hull.

In fact I hadn't a clue where Hanford Drewitt was, though it was close by at 241 Portage Avenue. "Western Canada's Finest Specialty Store" was foreign territory to a kid whose mom bought him clothing at Kmart. And although he appeared to be late for an appointment, he listened patiently as I stammered "I, um, I know you. Hello, um, Mr. Hull." The conversation that followed however, is etched in my memory. After all, I was having an actual conversation with one of the greatest hockey players of all time!

We discussed my hockey experience. He told me about his kids also playing (Bob Jr. and future Hall of Famer Brett Hull!), as well as Blake Hull, two years my junior. I told Mr. Hull that I was disappointed he couldn't play in the 1972 Canada/Russia Summit Series, and asked if he was surprised at how skilled the Russians were. "If you think they're good, wait until you see the Swedes," he replied. The following year he was playing with Ulf Nilsson and Anders Hedberg. And I was among the first Winnipeg fans to hear about their recruitment!

Then before I knew it, he thanked me and went on his way. I smiled all the way home. But damn, I wished I'd thought to get his autograph!

A year later I ran into him again, this time he was attending the AAA All Star Day at the old Winnipeg Arena, where sons Bobby Jr. and Blake were playing. He was up in the stands, engaged in conversation with another man who I assumed was also a hockey dad.

"We met before, by the Autumn Stone" I began. "Hey Guy, nice to see you" he quickly replied (I learned later he called everyone whose name he couldn't remember, "Guy"). Then after signing my program, he handed it to the other gentleman, whose brows furrowed as he signed it and handed it back. I'm sure he noticed the quizzical look in my face. He may have been a veteran of four NHL original six hockey teams, but I still had no idea who Winnipeg Jets Captain Ab McDonald was.

I would go on to play goal at the AA level, and once attended hockey school with Blake Hull, (who I recall borrowed a quarter from me to buy a chocolate bar. He never paid me back.) Blake's famous father never did come to the final intersquad game at the end of the week, but his mother did. There was no mistaking Joanne Hull in the stands, with her finely coiffed hair and fur coat. She wore oversized sunglasses as I recall. Indoors? We were too young, too idealistic, to think it was anything but ostentatious.

The last time I saw Bobby he was long retired, signing autographs at an old-timers game. I introduced my son Christian to him, and Bobby signed his hockey jersey. "Enjoy the game," he said. Looking at Christian, maybe seven at the time, he added "You too, Guy."

As we walked away, I looked back. There was a man whose life was hockey. Who lived for the game. Who, inarguably, was an icon of the game. Who has told and retold some of the funniest stories of the game. And though he smiled his famous smile with everyone he met, I felt a sadness I couldn't put my finger on.

Christian pulled my hand. "Who was that man?" He asked.

"He used to play for the Jets" I replied. "He was one of the best players ever. Had a slapshot over a hundred miles an hour... like a bullet."

"He's old," said Christian. "Like Grandpa."

I met Bobby Hull at Portage and Kennedy Street in 1973; 50 years ago and only five blocks from where he signed the first million dollar contract in hockey history. He brought pro hockey to the best fans in the country. He was a hero to many, and will live forever as #9, the Golden Jet, in hockey history.

Robert Marvin Hull died January 30, 2023, at the age of 84.

Maurice "The Rocket" Richard

He was fierce, flamboyant, and tempestuous. Eighteen seasons with the Montreal Canadiens; he was the first to score 50 goals in 50 games. People loved him or they hated him. He held 16 NHL records when he retired in 1960 – the year I was born.

He was not my dad's favourite player. Richard was, in his estimation, a bit of a dirty and reckless player. Dad preferred Jean Béliveau, a gentleman player, big and strong and gifted. "If you are going to model yourself after someone it should be Béliveau." I imagine my dad said that countless times during *Hockey Night in Canada*. And sometimes, on cold winter nights playing street hockey with my friend Glenn, I pretended to be Béliveau. I was, in fact, a very timid person then. But stories of Richard's exploits took my imagination elsewhere.

I played my first game of organized hockey (outdoors, thank you very much) in 1972. I was horrible; couldn't skate very well, couldn't skate backwards at all… but I had "heart" for the game. I persevered. By the end of that year I was skating with the first line; few goals (if any), but I could skate fast by then, and backchecking became my game. I imagined myself as Richard by then, but I could never score.

At an outdoor tournament in February of 1973, the Richard in me reared up. I took one too many slashes to my unprotected Achilles tendon, and lost it. I spun around and threw a punch to the face of the offending player; the only time in my life I have ever done that. The kid dropped to the ice with broken teeth and a split lip that would require stitches. I was suspended for the balance of the tournament, and left the ice to cries of "Monster!" by the mother of a teammate. My dad, watching from the other side of the rink, turned and walked home. The next weekend he took me ice fishing as I was still suspended… I don't think he was ever prouder of me, though he wouldn't say so at the time. I caught a seven pound Jackfish that he had mounted. It still hangs in my rec room.

I did see Richard play though, at an NHL Old-timers game in 1969. Afterward in the bowels of the old Winnipeg Arena my dad called out to Richard as he was leaving the dressing room. I was petrified. What would he say or do? Dad spoke with him for a few minutes and he signed my program. No idea what they spoke about. I still have the program to this day.

Almost 30 years later I reciprocated; took my dad to an NHL Old-timers game. This time Richard was the celebrity referee. There were many stars of the 70s and 80s playing and I was really enjoying the game, but Dad was distracted the entire time – commenting on people's dress, hair, attitudes... I was confused as I thought he enjoyed hockey, though he never had much time to watch me play. He later told me he never liked hockey (or the fact that I played), just the one player, Jean Béliveau, and his unlikely gentlemanly demeanor.

I convinced him to accompany me to the dressing room area after the game to have Richard sign an old book I brought, *Rocket Richard,* by sportswriter Andy O'Brien. I was disappointed when he brushed by, twice, accompanied by his handlers. It was a depressing night.

The book then became a reminder of this horrible evening for me.

One day in 1995, I sent the book to the Canadiens organization with the explanation of what had happened. "It is a valuable book" I wrote, "Perhaps you should give it to a real Habs fan who would appreciate it". I was actually relieved to get rid of it.

Two months later the book was returned to me with an apologetic letter, and a new inscription inside, pictured below. Maurice Richard died five years later, with a hero's funeral. I guess I will always be a Habs fan.

ROCKET RICHARD

By ANDY O'BRIEN

Bittersweet memories

I wanted so badly to play the drums. I tapped my fingers incessantly on the desk at school to the current song of the day, until I was sent into the hall for being a distraction. I did the same during lunchtimes at home, though I dared not do it at supper for fear of upsetting my dad. And though my mom put up with her "fidgety" son, it was Dad who wanted me to be a drummer. In fact, the only concert he ever took me to was at the Winnipeg Concert Hall in 1973, for a glorious evening with Buddy Rich and his big band. We had second row seats, and I was completely transfixed the entire show. And when it was over, Dad went up to the stage and boldly asked a drum tech for a souvenir stick. I still have it.

Shortly after, Dad allowed me to set up my blue sparkle Coronets in the living room for the purpose of regaling my visiting grandmother with Rich's Dancing Men, some seven minutes of impossibly fast jazz, played to the record on a very 1970s style consul stereo. My properly Mennonite grandmother had never heard such a bombastic cacophony, and along with most Mennonites of her day would likely have deemed it "devil music". But she survived and never held it against me. To this day I think Dad had his own reasons for subjecting her to this.

My sister Bonnie wanted to learn guitar, so just after her 13th birthday she got a sparkly blue electric guitar for Christmas. I was over-the-moon happy for her, until I opened my present… a tabletop hockey game. I was devastated, but got over it when Bonnie allowed me to play her guitar. Nothing could, or would ever compare to the gift of rock 'n' roll! She hadn't wanted an electric one anyway, and for the short period of time until it was traded for an acoustic, I got to play with it. Two long years later it was my turn, and when I saw the blue sparkle Coronets in the living room on Christmas morning in 1972, well, all was forgiven!

PHASE -5

Performing Friday, July 25th
Holiday Inn Ballroom
Following Mardi Gras Events

Allen Barrett, Mark Brooks, John Vagi, Bill Peters, Joe Costellano

All Have Studied With United Conservatory of Music

One of Winnipeg's Young "Up and Coming Bands"

DON'T MISS THEM!!

WILLIAM J PETERS

I practised, and I practised, and practised some more. I played before breakfast, when I came home for lunch, and for hours every evening. It consumed me until it became my identity. I had drums. I was a drummer!

In the fall of 1974, Harold Sokyrka, a representative of the United Conservatory of Music knocked on our front door, offering lessons in guitar, piano, and accordion. I stood behind my dad, listened to the pitch, and proudly nodded when Dad said "My son is a drummer". Harold looked at me and said "We don't teach drums, but have a combo program that needs a drummer. If you are interested, there would be no charge." He said just the right thing. The following Sunday afternoon, Mom drove me to the rehearsal space at 883 Notre Dame, and I met the guys who I would play with for the next four years — Allan Barrett, Joe Castellano, John Vagi, and Mark Brooks. We would collectively be known as *Phase 5*.

The Conservatory hosted an annual music competition, and in 1975 it was held at the Winnipeg Convention Centre. Phase 5 both competed, and "entertained" in one of the ballrooms.

We also competed as members of a concert band, my favorite part of the weekend. Guitars, bass, accordions, five singers, and me in the middle of it all. We played a medley of 60s hits, ending with *The Night has a Thousand Eyes* by Bobby Vee. We finished to thunderous applause, and shortly after were presented with a grand champion trophy. It was one of my proudest moments! We celebrated like we'd won the Stanley Cup, and kids from the other groups (and their parents) came to congratulate us for our win. It was absolutely euphoric. The best of times!

We separated for the rest of that summer, and got back together in September, less Mark Brooks. We did add another guitar player for a short time, named Alex, but the core group remained Joe, Al, John, and me. No longer a five-man group, we changed our name to

Bittersweet. We rehearsed on Sunday afternoons, alternating between Joe's family home on Margaret Avenue in the North End, and our home on Riel Avenue in St. Vital. We played a few gigs including an Italian christening, our manager Clark Tauber's wedding, and a disastrous appearance at Manisphere in front of Winnipeg Arena, where my snare broke on the very first song.

Our most memorable gig was a teen dance at Hedges Junior High in St. James. We pulled out all the stops. We rented lights – two banks of three (red, blue and green). We had two washtubs packed with dry ice, and some fans to blow the "smoke" over us for the requisite playing of *Smoke on the Water*. I think we even had a strobe light for my drum solo. Joe unbuttoned his shirt to expose his unusually hairy chest and his gold chains. He had naturally curly brown hair; a younger version of fellow Italian Gino Vanelli, and was the sole vocal, and focal point, of the band. Al occasionally made a song introduction, but John and I remained silent. It was no different on this night.

Then it happened. A small group of girls were staring at me, and in between songs started a chant along the lines of "Say Something! Say Something!" I waved at them and we played another song. Then another chant. "Say Something! Say Something!" It was surreal. Joe handed me the microphone, and all I could think to say was "Uh, hi". They exploded into cries of "Oh my God!" (I swear I am not making this up.) For that one moment in time, in June of 1975, I was at once a rock star and sex symbol. By the time we left I had received a proposal or two, lost all the buttons on my shirt to my "fans", lost several pairs of drum sticks, and almost lost

Ken Haller's cool lumberjack jacket, which I had borrowed to look even more cool than I apparently was. The boys had to pull me into the van while I pulled the jacket back from a fan. It was a Beatles moment I will never forget!

But as they say, what goes up must come down. At our next gig at my junior high alma mater, my drum solo was augmented with a super-cool flip toss of my drum sticks to an adoring crowd, after which I played with bare hands. Following lukewarm applause, a young lady asked for my attention. "You dropped these," she said, and gave me back my sticks. And so the memories, like the band, were bittersweet.

In the years since, I have reconnected with Al, who Olivia affectionately calls "Uncle Al", and Joe, the North End Italian Stallion who has settled in of all places, Winkler, Manitoba. I've lost track of John, however I still think of these guys as my brothers. And I'll never forget the night we were The Beatles.

Ladies with hats

The 1970s. The St. Mary's bus slows to a halt at Eaton's, where the proper ladies shop. I rub the condensation from the window, exposing a tableau now etched in echoic memory, triggered these days by, of all things, the hissing of air brakes.

Old ladies with hats.

Hats of felt or velvet; decorated with feathers, rhinestones and beads. Hats that matched clutches or purses. Perfect accessories for coats of fur, wool, or cashmere. Not utilitarian, but the kind of hats that make the statement "I'm a lady. I'm going shopping."

I inhale and my lungs humidify the dry Winnipeg winter air. I blow, and the tableau slowly fades to white frost. I knew in my heart at that moment that I would someday recall this exact moment in time, and miss it dearly. Today is that day.

The circle game

Heard Bachman Turner Overdrive's *Hey You* on classic radio recently. It still brings goosebumps.

But the BTO song that really gets my motor running has always been *Not Fragile*, sung by the inimitable C.F. (Fred) Turner.

Belted out at a 1975 Bachman Turner Overdrive concert, these words may have been lost on this 15-year-old, but their "heavy music" sound would inspire me, and ring in my ears decades later.

1975 was a pivotal year for my band. "Phase 5", as we were called, had been together for about a year. Of course we only played cover songs; even we knew our limited life experiences were little fodder for song. Our catalogue was limited to songs penned in the late 50s or 60s; from the rocking *Johnny B. Goode* to *Nights in White Satin*, and of course the BTO radio hits of the day, *Hey You* and *Takin' Care of Business*.

The core members of the band met in 1974 through the combo program at the United Conservatory of Music. We practised in a small studio at 883 Notre Dame on Sunday afternoons. A year or two later we would alternate between Joe's home in the North End on Margaret, and my home on Riel Avenue in St. Vital. Our goal, at least initially, was to compete in UCoM's annual band competition, in July of 1975. And with the new release of *Takin' Care of Business* in our repertoire, we won.

A week later I was in Churchill, Manitoba, where I would work for the rest of the summer pumping gas and fixing truck tires. Through the Conservatory I'd met Debbie, and we corresponded for a few weeks like I was off to war; both looking forward to my return, and the BTO concert in September.

We went to the concert together, but my attention was solely on BTO. Their music resonated with me. I played along with many of their albums in my basement bedroom... closing my eyes, and imagining that I was touring with the band. The feeling was indescribable. It resonated then, and it still does 40 years later.

Fred and me

At 59, I still play. Last year, in need of some cymbal stands, I responded to a Kijiji ad for tour quality hardware. The correspondence was brief and to the point:

Stands still available?
Yeah.
Reason for selling?
They belong to my son. He doesn't need them anymore and they are taking up space.

We wrote back and forth several times, confirming details and a time to get together that would suit us both. Each time, he signed his correspondence with F. Turner. I had to ask...

I hope you don't mind me asking... Does the F stand for Fred?
Yeah.
So you're "the" Fred Turner?
Yeah.

My daughter Olivia came along with me the next day. I tried hard not to geek out, but I don't believe I was very successful. Olivia would agree on that assessment, as I couldn't stop talking about Fred Turner and BTO all the way home!

We were idiots

I have often said that the title of my autobiography would be "We Were Idiots". I like the collective *we* as it infers shared blame; *I Was an Idiot* leaves no room for this. What follows is a story of shared blame for what is probably the most idiotic thing I have done in my life.

It was 1975. I was an inexperienced 15-year-old, and the opportunities for a summer job were limited. So when I was offered the chance to work in Churchill, Manitoba alongside my namesake cousin from Moose Jaw, Saskatchewan, Billy Robb, I took it. Billy, 16, had worked there the previous summer and was returning for the full two months of summer. Our Uncle Lorne, who was the town administrator, owned Hudson Motors where Billy worked. Lorne arranged for me to learn to fix tires and pump gas for the competition across the street. I would be there for a month.

It was Billy and his boss's 10-year-old son who picked me up at the airport, in a brand new 3/4-ton Chevy Silverado. Billy and I had not seen each other in over a year, and he was as excited to drive the truck as he was to show me around. And so off we went to the town dump... to look for polar bears.

There are no shortages of polar bear stories from the Churchill locals. They will tell you about the Polar Bear Alert Program, break-ins with doors and windows smashed, the garbage cans and cars/trucks pushed over, polar bear jails, and freezers full of arctic char ripped open like tin cans. Parents armed with high-powered rifles accompanying their kids as they trick or treated on Halloween. You name it, the 10-year-old had heard it all. And he was not about to let us get within a mile of a bear. But we were teenagers and he was ten, so off we went.

We arrived at the town dump about ten minutes from town, joined a group of two or three cars and craned our necks to see what they were using binoculars to see. And sure enough, about a half-mile away, there were three bears poking around in the garbage. I encouraged Billy to get a little closer, a sentiment that was met with absolute admonishment from the kid. *"NOOO! We can't! They'd kill us! Please! Take me home!"*

It was all noise where we were concerned. We took him home and returned the truck. Billy then produced a second set of keys to his ride, a 1972 Chevrolet Vega. We knew where we were going!

I guess the other folks at the dump got tired of looking at the bears as they were nowhere to be seen upon our return. But the bears were still there and appeared oblivious to the bright yellow Vega slowly approaching. Billy and I were dead silent, as though the bears couldn't already hear the four-cylinder engine slowly getting louder. And they didn't even look up, at least until we were less than 40 feet away.

There were three things we both knew to be true:
1. Never get between a mother bear and her cubs.
2. The bears were comprised of one mother and two cubs.
3. We were not *between* them, we were "alongside".

I wish I had a picture of Billy the moment I told him I was going to open the door and stand outside the car. I reasoned, "They aren't even LOOKING at us!" The mother bear did look up briefly with the click of the door opening, but continued to paw at something more interesting, or perhaps more edible, in the three-foot pile of garbage between us. And then there I was, standing outside the car, some 30 feet from a mother polar bear and her two cubs.

You might think I did not have a plan B if the bears started towards me, but I did. With my left hand on the door at all times, I'd jump in, in one precise motion, and my intrepid driver would floor it and whisk us away to safety. We'd smile nervously until we left the dump, leaving the bears in our dust while they returned to their previous activity. Then we'd laugh all the way home to Uncle Lorne's house to relate the story of our bravado.

What I did not plan on was Billy getting out on his side of the car.

This reminds me of the saying, "You don't have to be able to outrun the bear if you can outrun your friend." It was years later that I learned that a fully grown polar bear can crush a car like a tin can. And we were in a Chevy Vega.

I did not have to ask Billy to get back in the car, at least not verbally. I am sure Billy wishes that he had a picture of MY face at that moment. We quietly got in the car and left, with BIG smiles on our faces. The smiles of two young boys who'd just created a life story. A FANTASTIC and true life story that could only have been created by two, well, idiot teenagers.

A story that we kept to ourselves when we got back to town, and that I only told my uncle some 40 years later.

Sykotherapy

Our first response was to laugh; as one does when nervously anticipating the unknown...

Gym class at Dakota Collegiate was for lifting weights or climbing ropes, perhaps learning the finer points of basketball and dodgeball. "Boys Only" of course — we had little to do with the girls on the other side of the curtain that divided the gym in two. This class was to be different, and for me, life-changing. No Mr. Dale Bradshaw for this gym class; on this particular day we were going to have Ms. June Syko teach the boys... how to dance. Or more specifically, waltz.

This news precipitated brief panic among the 20-odd young bucks assembled. At first we eyed each other nervously, worried we might be paired off and forced to dance with each other. That would never happen. I'm not sure we heard anything Ms. Syko said in her introductory remarks; we were unaccustomed to being paid attention to by anyone so, dare I say it, beautiful.

And she was, there's no denying it. An athletic California blonde as far as we were concerned. Could have been a beach volleyball champion, or maybe a Dallas Cowboy Cheerleader with a smile as bright and youthful as Olivia Newton-John. Or a *Baywatch* lifeguard. Or all of the above... it didn't really matter. We all imagined her in our own post-pubescent testosterone-charged way.

Our imagining all ground to a halt when she barked "You!" and pointed through the gangly cast of characters in tight shorts and sweats to the one person in the class who had not heard a single word of her preamble. Pushed forward from the back row by my classmates with sniggering "Attaboy Peters" comments, I had no idea what she wanted me to do. I edged forward — there was no going back.

June Syko

More preamble. "The box step is named after the pattern it makes on the floor, which is just that, a square box. It can be applied to several dances, including the rumba, or even the fox trot." There was no nodding of agreement or understanding by anyone; we knew squat about such things. Say "Fox Trot" to a teenage boy in 1977 and not much sank in beyond the word "Fox"; like saying "Squirrel!" to a dog.

"Now take my right hand with your left."

THAT got their attention. All eyes were on me, as I instinctively raised my right hand, which I started to move awkwardly across to her waiting hand. A quick shift of her eyes and I autocorrected. "Not quite so tight!" she continued. "Keep your fingers together, but not stiff. And cup your hand slightly. Now put your right hand around my waist." I obliged... from about a foot away.

You could have heard a pin drop. I was, for that brief moment, suspended in time.

The moment that followed, however, would be a memory that would live vividly in my mind for more than 40 years. It is a film clip without a soundtrack, save the collective gasp of the boys...

"TIGHTER! Like THIS!" And just like that I was chest-to-chest and nose-to-nose with June Syko.

Beyond that moment I really don't remember much. We learned to box step in a stilted and graceless manner, stomping the square pattern with almost military precision. We learned to polka the same way — thankfully without ever having to partner up with one of the guys.

Of course the purpose and highlight of the exercise was "The Dance", where we were assigned partners from the girls' class. I really did enjoy that class, even though dancing is admittedly not something that comes naturally to me.

But it wasn't the highlight of 1977 for me. Not by a long shot.

Community club dance

In the 1960s, the heart of Winnipeg communities was the Community Club.

Greendell Community Club started out as a hockey rink and a tiny warm-up shack with a potbelly woodstove for heat. Supervision (if there was any) was by volunteer — often men with flasks of "antifreeze" in the vest pocket. To no one's surprise our shack burned down and was replaced in the early 70s by a modest structure just large enough to accommodate teen dances.

The first time I ever danced with a girl was traumatic. Grade 6 in Minnetonka Elementary; the beautiful Maryanne asked me to "slow dance", and pulled me tight to her chest. This (predictably) resulted in audible snickers from her band of friends lining the gym wall. You could have seen my sweat stains through a parka. For this, and a long list of reasons I will write about in the future, I abstained from asking girls to dance for years. Didn't stop me from attending the dances though, and then a life-changing musical moment at Greendell Community Club in 1973...

Teen dances meant live music, and on one occasion the drummer in the band broke his snare skin after only a few songs. They asked around and found that I was a drummer. I ran home and brought a replacement skin, hastily removed from my snare drum. It didn't occur to me to just bring the snare. They offered to pay, but I asked if instead I could "solo" on his kit on their break following the set. Kids usually left the building at that point for a smoke break, while the band hung out at the back door. The place would be nearly empty. The request was granted.

With my head down and my eyes closed, I started to play. The drums were far better quality than my own, and I was inspired to new heights. After a couple of minutes I opened my eyes. I was surrounded by about 80 stunned locals, most of which didn't know that I played, or certainly had never heard me play. They applauded loud and long, slapped me on the back, and treated me like a hometown hero.

It's been more than 40 years since, and I still think of Greendell Community Club as my "home club". Still don't like to dance.

Ode to #4

My first memories of *Hockey Night in Canada* were Saturday nights in the rec room of 200 Riel; curled up next to my dad with a bowl of popcorn. Seemed it was always Montreal vs. Toronto or Boston — didn't matter to me, as long as Montreal was playing. This was decades before the first iteration of the Winnipeg Jets, and as far as I was concerned Montreal was MY team. Dad would say to me, "Watch number 4. He's the best player in the NHL. That's Jean Béliveau."

There was no reason to doubt it; he really was the best. Tall, fast, soft hands... he seemed to score in every game. He was the captain. He was the first to be interviewed after each game, and the reporters would hang on every word. He was the first on the team to raise the Stanley Cup, which he did so many times. "But most of all," Dad would say, "He is a gentleman."

After the game I would beg to go out on the street to bat around a puck, scoring between two blocks of snow. On occasion my friend Glenn would come out to play, and we'd be forced to choose names. On the occasion when he called dibs for Béliveau I would be Jacques Plante — or perhaps Ken Dryden. But I preferred, when possible, to be Béliveau.

Of course I eventually did play organized hockey; a forward for two years, then a goaltender for six more. Mom drove me to most games/practices, and looking back Dad never really seemed to come as often as other dads did. It was years later that I learned he didn't like hockey. "I liked the man," he said, "not the game."

Jean Béliveau died a week ago; his funeral is tomorrow. I hope Dad gets to watch it on TV — I imagine he would say "Now THAT's a hockey player. He was the best."

WILLIAM J PETERS

Comedians in bars getting coffee

I spent my college years watching the folk trio Elias, Schritt and Bell in various bars around town. One night they were opening for a comedian from Toronto, who absolutely brought the house down with his impressions. After the last set, the ESB folks were deciding where to go for coffee. The comedian had no entourage and was waiting by the bar, presumably to be paid. I walked over and introduced myself, congratulated him on his set, and asked if he'd like to join us. He politely declined, and thanked me for the invitation. He said he had an early flight home the next day. It was probably the right decision, as we were out until at least 4:00 a.m.

That was the night I was turned down for a coffee date by Jim Carrey.

That time I almost killed a guy

I took a year off after squeaking through high school to play in a punk band and experience life. Of course Dad said I couldn't just lie around the house in my off- hours, so I found work and paid rent. I moved to full-time hours at Goodyear, as it had been my part-time gig throughout high school. That lasted through winter, then I was "let go" for reasons I can't remember, though I do recall the manager was an ass, so our working relationship was likely the reason. I moved through several jobs through the summer and into the fall, notably Cam Gard Electronics (shipper/receiver, fired) and Advance Electronics on Portage Avenue (service writer, fired). These were low paying jobs, but they kept the rent paid while I played in The Photoz. It was a fun year; playing socials and bars, hanging out, coming home at four in the morning. So much more fun than university was for many of my high school friends.

But the year passed and I enrolled with a full course load (Economics, Political Science, Psychology, Sociology and Advanced French) at the University of Winnipeg in the fall of 1979. That crashed and burned by Christmas, and in January I started as guitars/drums manager at Hildebrand Music & Jewellery in Steinbach, and taught drum lessons at their Winnipeg location (Southwood Mall) on Friday nights. I was a bit of a local celebrity in Steinbach, having been announced in the Steinbach *Carillon* as a "professional drummer from Winnipeg." High school girls would drop by to look at me, then giggle and wander off. Despite not selling a single instrument in three months I was promoted to store manager at the North Kildonan location in Winnipeg, where I was equally unsuccessful. I did, however, teach myself to play some piano during those long and lonesome days. I was fired and brought to small claims court on a theft charge after they noticed a bass guitar missing from stock. I had loaned it to a local musician for a month, as he couldn't afford to rent it and was recording a self-produced demo. The charge was thrown out, but so was I.

My high school friends were starting their second year.

My resumé was not particularly impressive at this point. Determined not to have to move home, and at the advice of my new brother-in-law Doug, I applied to work at Canada Packers. Wages there were much higher than I'd been making, and I was excited to start in the spring of 1980.

There was little orientation training at Packers. Outfitted with white pants and shirt, a bright yellow rubber apron, a "steel" (honing rod), a boning knife and ear plugs, I was dropped off in the pork department, a loud and busy production line where large chunks of pig are subdivided into recognizable cuts of meat. It was the start of a three-month probationary period, after which I could be accepted into the Union.

There was a distinct brotherhood evidenced at Packers; lots of nodding, winking, gesturing that I couldn't have identified on the first day. I also didn't know sharp from dull, and had no experience with a steel. My appointed supervisor offered to sharpen my knife when he saw me struggling, likely with a wink and nod to the guys on the line. They chuckled as I furiously sawed and hacked away, but their faces turned when I withdrew my left hand, dripping with blood at every heartbeat. That dulled knife had all but severed my pinky finger. I never worked with those guys again.

For the next month I worked "light duty"; anything that could be done with one hand. But as my left hand healed I moved around different departments, packing pork hocks, smoked meats, hot dogs (yes, I still eat them), and pretty much doing the least-liked jobs there. On the last day of my probationary period I was packing boxes onto pallets, stamping the date on them, and wrapping the loaded pallets with cellophane. I remember an older gentleman, perhaps in his mid-60s, making the rounds among guys in the area. He was shaking their hands and laughing. He came by to talk to me, told me that he was working his last day, and was retiring. He'd just come by to say his goodbyes. When I told him I was on my last day of probation he asked about my plans for the future. I told him I wanted to earn enough money to go back to school. "Is that right?" he said. Then he said something that I remember to this day:

"That's what I said 30 years ago."

After being accepted into the Union my salary went up to $9.75/hr., and I was told to report to the hog kill floor. The additional money did go to my head for a bit; after a few weeks I flew to Chicago for the weekend to visit my friend Cynthia, in fact I called in sick so I could catch my Friday morning flight. That trip culminated in a "kegger" party held at one of Cynthia's friend's apartment. The host, David, asked me about my job at Packers. I suppose in retrospect he was impressed by my being able to fly there just for the weekend. I spared him the gory details of my job (trimming blood-soaked fat from the hole where the pigs had bled out) and focused on my plans to return to school. I asked him where he was in his education, and he said he'd just been accepted to article with a local law firm, and that he'd be graduating in a year. It shouldn't have been, but it was like a gut punch from reality. I was still planning, while others were achieving, and the thought of my friends at home doing the same weighed heavily on my mind. When my mother asked how the trip went I said, "Fine. It was all good." Then I went for a walk. And I cried.

I would work at Packers for another year, salting away money so I could afford the tuition and books, as well as a car. I had lunch with 600 employees dressed in white coats with crimson red blood stains. The guys that worked in my section nicknamed me "sleepy", as I never did get used to starting work at 7:00 a.m. I had pig eyeballs thrown at me to intentionally draw my ire. One day when I'd had enough, I pushed an instigator against the wall, held him by his lapels, and told him I'd take it outside if he didn't stop. In my rage I forgot I was still holding a fourteen-inch knife in my right hand, and the blade was perilously close to his neck. He never bothered me again.

I was accepted into the Creative Communications program at Red River Community College in the fall of 1981. On the first day, we all took turns introducing ourselves. As most of my fellow students were right out of high school, there was not much to say. Then it was my turn.

"My name is Bill Peters. I took a year after school to play drums in a punk band. I was fired from several jobs before working on the kill floor at Canada Packers. I'm really looking forward to getting my life started."

At this writing, my 35-year career in corporate communications is done. But I still carry a finger scar as a reminder of my Packers days.

Daily takeout

In the winter we'd pick up the kids at daycare after work. Olivia hated her snowsuit, Christian not so much. But the best part was that their East Indian nanny was a fantastic cook, and their snowsuits soaked up the flavours during the day. When we loaded them in the van they smelled like takeout. Good times.

Olivia with Auntie Terry

The real veal deal

When I was in college I worked as a delivery driver for a Chinese restaurant. On each shift I was allowed one combination meal. I always ordered the one with dry breaded pork, as it was cheaper and I didn't want to appear to be ordering expensive meals. After two years I decided to treat myself to a graduation treat – the more expensive veal. "It's the same thing," they replied. "When it's breaded no one can tell."

Mary Tyler Moore

"Who can turn the world on with her smile?"

What a great line to be remembered by. I can't hear her name without that tune coming to mind.

"Who can take a nothing day, and suddenly make it all seem worthwhile?"

Mary Tyler Moore

I met MTM on February 24, 1997. She was speaking at Winnipeg's Centennial Concert Hall and I was hired to take backstage pictures. There were many VIP's at the post-talk reception, and in the pre-cell phone era if you had a Nikon camera around your neck you were pretty popular with those who wanted a "selfie" with the star. In fact, many of the women attending the reception were downright chummy with me, perhaps hoping they'd be in the *Free Press* the next day. I was hired by the St. Boniface Hospital Foundation, so that wasn't going to happen. But I enjoyed their attention anyway.

I wasn't shooting digital pictures in those days, only film. And my Vivitar flash just chewed through batteries. It was while I was changing the film/batteries when a woman approached me with some concern. "You look exhausted," she said. "Is everything alright?"

I took a few seconds to explain that my wife has just got home that day from the hospital, having given birth by C-section to my son only five days earlier. There had been a few sleepless nights, as well as the stress of preparing for this night. "Hey Mary... Your photographer and his wife just had a baby — their first boy!" she said. Mary was a scant ten feet away.

Mary had just stopped speaking with a fan and turned her attention to me. "Well congratulations! A boy? What's his name?" she asked. I told her his name (Christian) and that he had just come home from the hospital that day.

Her attention, and that of everyone around her, was on me. She then asked that I go ahead and take some pictures so that I could go home and be with my family. Something about me having a son seemed to ring true with her; it was much later that I learned she had lost her first son in a gun accident some years earlier.

The picture accompanying this story is the only one I took of her by herself, shortly after she congratulated me on the birth of my son.

Thanks Mary. You will be missed.

A brief eternity in Pine Falls

(A tale of amoxicillin, hydroxyzine, and prednisone vs. sage, cedar, and muskeg tea)

Olivia at the lake

Our family spends a week of summer vacation at the Peters family cottage on Lake Winnipeg. I always take the camera along — to take pictures of the kids mostly, but also to take pictures of a variety of hummingbirds, deer, flowers, etc. One hot mid-afternoon I was showing my daughter Olivia how to choose foregrounds for artistic pictures when we stumbled upon a great photo opportunity. I had Olivia sit on a rock and look out at the lake while I knelt low in the foxtails to shoot a picture of her. With natural backlighting through the leaves of a nearby oak tree, I had my picture.

Later that afternoon while working on a sign for our cottage, I noticed an itchy patch of skin on my leg, perhaps an inch in diameter. I wrote it off as a scratch from the wood I was chiseling. By the next morning however, I had throbbing pain in my leg. It had grown to four inches, and was thick as a pancake — with a black spot that looked like mould forming in the center.

Of course I became worried I had contracted some kind of flesh-eating disease. I'd never experienced anything like this in my life, and I must admit I am just a bit of a hypochondriac in this regard. I didn't want to cut our vacation short with a return to a Winnipeg specialist, so I decided we'd drop in to Pine Falls Hospital, about 40 kilometres in the opposite direction.

Pine Falls is a very small mill town situated on the edge of the Fort Alexander First Nation Reserve. Forty kilometres is a LONG drive for a hypochondriac, and much longer when you notice other parts of both legs have become itchy as well. Fortunately the kids blessed me with their patience and consideration, and didn't whine about the vacation detour, at least once I told them there would be chocolate bars in Pine Falls...

By the time we got there I was prepared for bad news, but had a brave face for my wife and kids. We went to the hospital and were told there'd be a wait. After that brief eternity, I was seen by the doctor.

"You have a localized infection. I will prescribe antibiotics, a steroid, and an antihistamine." "Yes, but what caused this?" I asked. "I

cannot say, but you do have an infection, and we will treat it as such." Then he was gone, and I was alone with my thoughts, which I might add is not necessarily a good thing.

Moments later, a nurse arrived to put a dressing on my infection. Where the doctor had the appearance and accent of foreign origin, (often rural doctors are from other countries) she was obviously a local and possibly from the neighbouring reserve. She went quietly about her job. When I asked if it was poison ivy, she looked at my leg, then toward the door, then back at me. *"You have what looks like poison ivy above and below the infection, and on your other leg as well. We see this all the time. It's going to itch for awhile. Don't scratch it."*

Poison ivy — what a relief! In only a few words and with some sympathy, she had set my mind at ease. And it made sense to me that, as a local woman, she had likely seen this many times from the hunters and fishermen of the area. Probably had it herself at one time. She was gone before I could properly thank her. The doctor returned with his prescription, asked me to start as soon as possible, and follow up with my doctor if it got worse.

Poison ivy itches like nothing else. Within a week I'd scratched it to five or six different locations on both legs, and was researching incessantly on the web for relief, but to no real avail. I remembered the calm advice of the nurse. Then it occurred to me that perhaps I was looking in the wrong place.

Winnipeg is home to thousands of First Nations people, and has a healing centre called Thunderbird House only a few miles away from where I work. I contacted Linda — an Elder with a very calming, spiritual demeanor, much like I'd experienced with the nurse in Pine Falls. She said she'd see me right away, but to be sure to bring a gift of tobacco — customary when asking Elders for advice (try finding tobacco in a hospital these days). Thunderbird House has the aura of a church sanctuary. I removed my shoes and walked across a beautiful hardwood floor. Linda met me at the door of her office — simply but beautifully decorated with Indigenous art, pictures of friends and grandchildren, an eagle feather, and a cupboard she laughingly referred to as her medicine cabinet. She accepted the two cigarettes I had obtained (thanks Dr. H, you really should quit) as my gift and placed them into a basket with a variety of small bags of tobacco.

We talked about the poison ivy, and where I may have come into contact with it. Linda went into her cupboard and measured out three small baggies of hand-picked sage, cedar, and muskeg tea, with instructions to boil and strain it, then apply with a clean cloth three times daily. Her instructions were precise, and she told me to write them down. *"Also,"* she said, *"when you add each bag to the water you must thank the Creator for the ingredient, and say that it is for curing the poison ivy on your legs. OK?"* She continued — *"And if you can, get about two pounds of earth from the area where you got the poison ivy and make a paste with clean water that you can apply and let dry, once a day. That should do it. Call me in a couple of days and let me know how it goes."*

Whatever skepticism I may have felt was allayed by Linda's sincere concern for my uncomfortable condition. I must admit I didn't write the instructions down and screwed up by soaking my ankle in the solution for an hour instead of dabbing with a cloth as instructed (she gave me three more baggies). After a few days the itching subsided, and eventually the sores dried up.

The internet has revealed some interesting treatment options, though most sufferers seem to end up letting the disease run its course. What this experience has taught me, however, is that the stress caused by the unknown was the worst part of the experience. And that two First Nations women helped give me a new way of looking at the delivery of healthcare.

And for that I am tremendously thankful.

A Christmas tale

One of my favourite Christmas memories was when Christian was four and heavily into the movie *Toy Story*. Christmas shopping was a breeze that year; anything from that movie would send him over the moon. And there was no end to the merchandising; it would only require a quick trip to Walmart and I'd be done.

There was a whole aisle dedicated to Buzz and Woody, but to my slight dismay there were no matching sets for these characters. No matter, I found a great articulating Woody, and a slightly plusher Buzz Lightyear that would kind of go together. Topped them off with a pair of Woody "There's a snake in ma boots" onesie pyjamas and I was gold.

Of course we got both kids too much that year, and for Christian the toys were a hit. And to this day that's really all that matters.

Later that day we packed up the kids and headed to Mom and Dad's for the annual Peters Family Christmas evening, as was our tradition. We did not allow the kids to take any of their presents with them, as they'd be getting more from Grandma and Grandpa anyway.

Uncle Bob, eager to share in their Christmas joy, asked Christian what he got for Christmas that morning. And with a great big smile, Christian uttered the words that I fully expect Bob to retell again this year – because it always makes us laugh.

"I got a soft Buzz, and a hard Woody"

The value of a dream

My son's bedroom is a place to sleep to be sure — but more importantly, it is also a place to dream.

When I was his age, I dreamed of playing in the NHL, and my dream team was the early 1970s Montreal Canadiens. Though my dad never played hockey, he recognized the value of a dream, and he sat through every *Hockey Night in Canada* broadcast with me — even told me his favourite player was Jean Béliveau, and encouraged me to emulate him in the way I played. He nailed hockey sticks to the ceiling of my bedroom, and encouraged me to believe in that dream.

Now my son is seven and brings home books from school like *Number Four, Bobby Orr*. I read to him from Andy O'Brien's book on Rocket Richard. And on Saturday night when the theme from HNIC comes on, he yells "Dad! Hockey!" and curls up with me to watch whoever's playing. He straps on the pads and I take shots at him during commercials. By the end of the game he's sleeping in my arms and I carry him up to bed.

Christian's room reflects three things: his love for hockey, my love for him, and his for me. At the incentive of this competition we completed his room in one week, in Canadiens colours. He painted, nailed, and designed right alongside me. This NHL room has brought father and son together like nothing else can.

It is not the destination that counts — it's the journey. I never made the NHL, but I'd never deny the dream of my son. Even if that dream is feeding the perfect assist to the Rocket!

WILLIAM J PETERS

Christian in his Canadiens-themed bedroom

The milkman

We had new neighbours. Deb and Mary Anne had moved directly across the street, and it appeared they were in the process of cleaning and upgrading Stan and Jean's 1960s bungalow. I had introduced myself to Deb only a few days before, but on this day a slightly distraught Mary Anne smiled shyly and walked to the edge of her driveway. "Is there any chance you have a spare key to our house?" she said. "I've locked myself out, and we only have one key."

And so I did as one does in these circumstances, and joined Mary Anne in staring at the locked door. I tried the handle. Yep, it was locked all right. As were all the windows. There was no way in. The only exception was a tiny "milk door". Mary Anne opened the door and I peered in to their kitchen. So near and yet...

In 1950s and 60s Winnipeg, home milk delivery from local dairies was commonplace, and many houses had built-in milk doors that facilitated the regular transfer of fresh milk to the kitchen. Just high and wide enough for milkmen to pick up empty bottles and leave fresh ones, they were too small to get through and consequently were rarely, if ever, locked. They reminded me of 1930s gangster movies, where someone would give the secret knock, and a door would slide open. Then a quick transfer of cash through the opening, or a secret password exchange. Much to my disappointment, our house on Riel didn't have one. And this actually presented an unforeseen problem. Milkmen didn't have the time to knock and wait at every door, so if there was no milk door they'd just knock and leave the milk on the back doorstep. And our doorstep faced south, so if mom didn't hear the knock, the milk would sit in the sun.

Back in the 1960s the remedy for this situation was simple. Our door was never locked, so Charlie, our milkman for many years, just knocked, opened the door, and in his distinctly tenor voice yelled "milkman!" He then proceeded into our kitchen to put the milk on the table, or sometimes directly into the fridge. Problem solved.

For so many reasons, this would never happen in today's Winnipeg.

As a youngster I often imagined myself wriggling through these doors; a Houdini trick limited to skinny kids like me. In the moment I peered through the door into Mary Anne's kitchen, I had solved the dilemma.

He was reluctant at first, but when I told him he was our only hope, my then 11-year-old son Christian stepped up. In headfirst and lowered by the ankles, he unlocked the door in seconds.

Problem solved!

Calling in reinforcements

We all learn parenting on the fly, and there have been times when I've needed outside help. This is pretty self-explanatory:

Letter from me:

Dear Mr. White,
Christian lied to me this morning about brushing his teeth. After confronting him about this, he said he would never do it again. Could you reinforce the importance of not lying, especially to parents? I would appreciate the help. He doesn't appear to think it was that important. He also lost his temper and broke a light switch. It will be an opportunity to teach him about the cost of such things, and the danger of losing his temper. I told him he would have to get this letter signed and return it to me. Thanks!

Letter I got back:

Hey Bill, sounds like a difficult start to your day. I will try to find an opportunity to encourage Christian to think about his actions. This is a regular part of our everyday devotions. Reflecting Christ in our daily actions. Take care, Greg.

Thanks Greg. For the record, I don't think he always brushes regularly.

But at least he doesn't lie about it anymore.

The nativity

Current Christmas preparations remind me of discourse that occurred about this time last year. A conversation I found hilarious; Roula not so much...

I am not a Christmas decorator. Don't get me wrong, I love the festive look from the front door wreath to the strings of light colouring the snow in the back yard. The obligatory Christmas tree, festooned with colourful bulbs, decorations collected since we married over 30 years ago, and topped with my sister-in-law's hand-stitched angel. The smell of scented candles burning, with lights down low to enhance their ambience. Everything unloaded from storage in the garage for about six weeks of enjoyment; the empty boxes returned to the garage awaiting reload in January.

And that was my job, to unload and reload the boxes. I enjoy watching the kids decorate, and Roula directing traffic.

I didn't know how upsetting it might be to add something to the mix, so I didn't think twice about accepting the gift of Mom's ceramic nativity set. Eleven hand-painted pieces masterfully designed to fit together on a cherry wood platter.

I fit it together the first time; three wise men and a shepherd in the back row, Joseph, Mary, an angel and a lamb in the middle, and in the front, baby Jesus in a manger flanked by a cow on one side and a donkey on the other. Easy-peasy, with no room to spare – only one configuration works. Jesus front and centre, with the historic supporting cast of characters around and behind. Ceramic perfection.

And so I watched last year as Roula eyed the eleven pieces and started arranging them. This is the conversation that ensued:

Roula: *I know I should know this, but...*

Me (looking down): *Tall ones in the back, short ones in the front.*

Roula (picks up manger): *I think this would look better in the corner.*

Some people wait years for this kind of comedic setup. I had to take a breath and compose myself. Then I uttered the line that will go down in Peters Family history:

Hey! No one puts baby Jesus in the corner!

And that, Patrick Swayze, is how you do it.

Dr. John

"It is with sad hearts and deep respect that we acknowledge the recent passing of Dr. John Foerster, former Executive Director of St. Boniface Hospital Research, and a veritable pillar in the academic, scientific research, medical and faith communities, both here at home, and internationally."

I read the subsequent story on my iPhone; published on the website I pioneered and beautifully written by my successor. I felt relief in its reading, knowing that I could not have performed this duty without many a tearful pause.

Dr. Foerster's professional accomplishments were many and of the highest order, from Head of Medicine (1975) to Director of Research (1987). Under his leadership the Centre flourished from a handful of staff to nearly 200, from one cardiovascular group in 1987 to several internationally prominent research teams in infectious diseases, respiratory medicine, nephrology, cardiology, clinical nursing research, cancer research, even sleep research! He was an esteemed member of many associations, winner of awards and honours including the Order of Canada.

I made my career supporting his vision; early on with overheads and slides, then graphics and PowerPoint presentations. I photographed him often, and my portraits of him were used in many of his publications, in award programs, on plaques honouring him at the Centre, and in newspaper articles. Every picture seen publicly portrayed him in a professional manner, of course, but the smile, or lack thereof, was often elicited by me — and those one-on-one interactions are now precious memories.

Dr. John Foerster

After I said "You're supposed to look professional." He replied "Don't I always?"

I loved having lunch with him. On one such occasion he drew a Venn diagram with three overlapping circles on a piece of paper. "This is the Research Centre, and this is the Hospital. Do you know what the third circle is? Clinical Research." Within a few years there was a $30 million clinical research institute on the campus.

Of course not all of his visions came true, or were successful... the Lions Manor Alzheimer's Disease project and the redevelopment of the south west part of the campus come to mind. But he never stopped dreaming of bigger and better. I recall Harry Schulz, then Director of Business Operations, saying "John, there is a fine line between being a visionary and seeing things." John's overall track record speaks for itself.

Of course all of his visions required A/V, and John asked for the moon on a paperboy budget. With his confidence and unwavering support, we produced many promotional videos in support of major projects, from the Age of Discovery campaign to the animated "donor ask" video for what is now the Asper Clinical Research Institute.

Despite his accomplishments, he was a humble, church-going family man. My first formal dinner date with Roula was a Christmas dinner at his house on Assiniboine, in 1989. For many years he took the administrative staff and their spouses to dinner at Hy's or Dubrovnik, at his personal expense. He personally bought (ok, Gisela may have helped) Christmas gifts for the staff. He told the funniest stories. Once, after closing down a social at 2:00 a.m., I went to the Centre to back up computer files and found him reviewing patient files at his desk. He cared so deeply about his cancer patients that we worried about him. He always delivered powerful talks to potential donors, and spoke to each and every one who wanted his time. His door was open. He had beautiful penmanship, and wrote detailed thank-you notes, signed "Affectionately, John." He loved being at the cottage, and absolutely loved and was proud of, his family. He was not fond of bears.

And I believe he cared about me more as a person than an employee.

Roula and Gisela had genuine affection for each other. She is missed too.

John wrote me a note a few years ago, which I framed and display proudly in our home. In it he says *"We always loved and admired your family, and I, of course, was so privileged to have Bill as an important and loyal coworker in building the St. B. research enterprise... May God bless you richly."*

John has meant so much to me, and is the standard I hold myself to in my professional and personal life.

I will miss him greatly.

Oh Henry

It was a hundred Christmas mornings rolled into one. And perfect timing too; I'd just rolled it off the trailer when Christian came home from school. He stood with me, staring.

"Is this yours?" he asked.

"It is now," I said, proudly.

"Where's the back window?"

In my excitement at finally landing Uncle Henry's 1968 Firebird 400, I hadn't noticed, though it had been there when I picked up the car at the Canada/US border. "I imagine it's in a thousand pieces on the highway," I replied.

This moment was the culmination of about 47 years of pining for this car, starting in the summer of 1968. I recall the moment; staring into the driver's side window at the bucket seats and standard shifter. "What do you think, Billy? Pretty nice, isn't she?" Uncle Henry said, washing the car on our front lawn. He sprayed me with the hose.

It was a far cry from our old station wagon, and the 1949 Mercury 1/2-ton Dad used for weekend tree jobs – they were entirely utilitarian; the Firebird an extravagance I could only imagine in my young life.

I'm certain my dad saw it differently. Uncle Henry was staying with us while attending the University of Manitoba, and Dad was proud that he was able to support Henry in getting his degree; as the youngest of eight boys and two girls, Henry was like a son to him. But he wasn't paying rent, and the Firebird was an extravagance he thought Henry shouldn't have afforded.

Many "car guys" have a list of cars they should have kept; cars that invoke youthful memories. For me it was a 1964 Chevrolet Impala SS convertible purchased in 1974. I put everything I earned into it before I sold it in 1981. Many great memories are attached to that car, and over the years I've often wanted it back. Henry, on the other hand, kept his Firebird and made a lifetime of memories in it. He had it when he got married, when he moved to Salinas, California, when he had kids, when he got his law degree, and when he got divorced. And when many years later he stopped driving it, he kept it in storage. I asked him about the car at my grandmother's funeral in 1994. "You wouldn't want it anymore. It is piled under boxes in storage, hasn't run for a few years, and it's starting to rust..."

I called Henry on his 70th birthday. After a few minutes of niceties he knew where the conversation was headed. "About the car," he started. My heart was in my throat. "I've realized I'm never going to get to it. So I've given it to John."

I immediately contacted my cousin John, an officer in the United States Navy. "Hi John. Saw the pic of the '68 in your Facebook photos. If you or your dad ever sell, I'm your man. Have been in love with that car since your dad used to wash it on our lawn."

John replied, "My father's '68 is in pretty sorry shape sad to say but even so I'm doing my best to keep her in the family and get her restored." I asked that he keep me in mind, and thought that would be the end of my quest.

And then, a year and a half later and on my 53rd birthday, I received this message from John:

"Happy birthday. Also I had been meaning to get ahold of you for a while but things keep coming up. I wanted to see if you were still interested in my dad's '68 Firebird. I really wanted to restore it myself and keep it in the family but with things the way they are that's just not working out. So if you are still interested let me know. I'll warn you though that car is in some pretty bad shape. It runs but most certainly would not make the drive to Canada. Look, we are family and as such I am happy with the money I'll save from not having to insure, register, and store it. You want it after you see the pictures you can have it." I was excited beyond words, and had SO many questions. What does it need? Is there a title? Do the brakes work? Does any of this matter? YES! I WANT THE CAR!

With John being stationed in the state of Washington, over 900 miles away from the Firebird, logistics became an issue. His mother had the keys to the storage unit. Should I fly there and hope to get the car in shape to drive it home? If I hired a transport company, could the arrangements be made without me physically being there? It would cost $1,600 to have the car shipped, and they wanted it running, with the brakes and emergency brake in working order. It would be too much to ask my aunt to take care of this. It was starting to be a frustrating process. So, if not Auntie Carol, who?

I didn't know anyone else in Salinas, but I did have a professional colleague in Fremont, CA, maybe 90 minutes away. And as luck would have it, Laurie's husband was an avid car guy. Enter my hero, Mr. Alan Lambert! The Lamberts road-tripped to Salinas to see if the car was worth salvaging. I waited and watched for their text. Alan confirmed that it was certainly worth salvaging (I learned later how subjective that call was), and that he would be happy to trailer the Firebird to Fremont so that he could get it running and the brakes working. I don't know if I could have done it any other way. Before loading up the car for its voyage across the country, Alan admitted he'd taken the car for a trip around his neighbourhood, and "maybe" burned a little rubber off the tires. I was happy to hear it!

And so the Firebird landed at Pembina, North Dakota, and after a lengthy discussion at Border Customs over its valuation, I paid the taxes and trailered the car home. And yes, somewhere along bumpy Highway 75 lay the thousands of pieces of OEM rear window glass, but I really didn't care. The Firebird was mine, and it was home!

The Firebird today

The Chrome Pit

As a car restorer I am more along the lines of a "decorator". I like to clean things, polish things, buy new things. Maybe change the oil in the driveway or shake out the air filter. I can do a few more things with the Firebird than I can with our main vehicle, (Ford Escape), but I tend to focus on what makes the car look good rather than function properly.

The hood on the car has removable air scoops, which were destined for chroming from the start. The challenge is finding a place to do this, as the by-products of chrome plating are inherently bad for the environment.

Today at lunch time I drove to the former Dominion Bridge yards to find the Chrome Pit; hidden in the recesses of the old plant. "Call me on the cell if you can't find us," the guy on the phone said, rather impatiently. I didn't have to do that, but it did take me 10 minutes to navigate the labyrinth of unused rail lines and machine sheds once through "Gate 4". It was like a movie set from the apocalypse; I half-expected a visit from the Warriors...

The door at the "customer entrance" had no knob, just an open padlock on a bar across the door. The acrid smell of metallic grime and acid baths was strangely welcoming. "Ya, whattaya got?... OK, 60 bucks. Each." No bartering here...

Then a man in a heavy apron appeared from the back room. His white hair was close-cropped and he had a mask over most of his face. I assumed from his skin colour that he was black, until he reached for the parts on the counter and I saw that his hands were white. I looked back at his face, then back at his hands. And back to his face again. He must have seen the quizzical look on my face, but if he thought anything of me I couldn't tell by his mask. He grabbed the parts and left me with the other man, who filled out the paperwork and sent me on my way. Looking forward to February 21st when I get my scoops back.

In the meantime I'm going to do some research on chemical causes of vitiligo...

Hit it!

Christian: *Hit it harder.*

Roula: *OK*

Christian: *Harder!!!*

Roula: *I've never hit something so hard in my life!* (Huge smile)

Olivia (to me): *That's probably a good thing...*

(Conversation at the first ever Peters Family Band rehearsal. Roula is our drummer.)

White on rice

So many money making opportunities coming by email these days...

My "friend" Wang Yongli, a Chinese investment banker with the renowned ICBC Bank, just contacted me through the internet, a medium which has been *"severely abused, but remains the fastest means of communication"*. Yongli guarantees *"100% rice and friendship transfer for the partnership and the entire counter"*, which I take to mean friendly rice all over my counter. Not sure I need that. She goes on to say *"The men are private, and they are able to respect the forces."* I am not sure what this means. I suppose the men who bring the rice are discreet; God forbid your neighbours find out that you have rice all over your counter and they do not. I love that they respect the Force, which I assume refers to Roula as she is generally in charge of the kitchen.

Anyway, having Canada's only rice-covered counter would bring me *"a total of 27 million euros in the most legal way"*.

I'd be all over this (like white on rice!) except we have a significant investment in granite counter tops, and "remove and replace" is not mentioned in her email.

There's always a catch.

Yay sports!

My personal sports "career" highlight was playing for the St. Vital Victorias AA hockey team for three years; one as a forward and two as a goalie. I think the best we ever did was just shy of a .500 season.

Fortunately, in sports, I get to live through Christian now.

Christian's varsity basketball team at Westgate Mennonite Collegiate just won the city AAA championship and will be competing in the provincials next weekend. Many of those kids won the city championship in AAA volleyball this year as well. They are an excellent group of boys in many ways, and he will miss playing with many of them when they graduate and he becomes a senior. Next year's group is very promising as well, and Christian will step into a larger role which will be exciting. Already looking forward to that!

Christian gave up hockey this year to become involved in high school sports, and I must admit I miss it at times. The last three years his AA team has made it to the city finals, and won twice. In the summers in between he focused on baseball, playing on two city/provincial champion AAA baseball teams. He has also played in two national championships where he has received several game star and MVP honours.

He plays men's league soccer in his spare time, plays guitar and drums equally well, and French horn in the high school concert band. He sings. He bugs me to take him snowboarding in the mountains, and tonight (on the way home from soccer) said bicycle ice cross would be fun to try.

The fact is, I prayed for a son like him, and a daughter like Olivia (much more on her another time). As they say, be careful what you wish for...

Sorry Dr. King

Back in 2006, I attended a professional meeting of the Health and Science Communications Association in Washington, DC. I was serving as association president at the time, and used the opportunity to have the family along, as my Hilton suite was covered by the association for a week. The facilities and hospitality were unparalleled.

We stayed for a few days after the meeting, visiting the Holocaust Museum, the Smithsonian National Museum of American History, the Air and Space Museum, and landmarks including the White House, Washington Monument, and the Lincoln Memorial, where 60 years ago Martin Luther King gave his "I Have a Dream" speech. Our visit literally ended with a bang; actually thousands of bangs at the Fourth of July fireworks display. The visit was memorable and inspiring.

On July 3rd of this year, I turned to Roula and said, quite matter-of-factly, "I wonder how many mass shootings there'll be on the Fourth of July?" as we've come to expect now.

"There's already been one," she replied.

As of this writing, there have been 14, including one where at least nine people, including a child and a teenager, were injured in a shooting in the nation's capital.

I'm glad we visited when we did, and fondly remember my good friend Lynn Povanda's excitement in hosting my family at the fireworks display.

Sadly, I don't think I'll ever return. It's just too dangerous. I have a dream too, and it involves living well into my retirement.

Pawan K. Singal

I'd just received a personal message regarding the passing of an old colleague and friend, cardiovascular researcher Dr. Pawan K. Singal, while preparing to leave on a motorcycle trip to the Black Hills with my brother Bob, and son Christian. The news hit me hard, as I'd just attended a retirement party a week earlier and no one even mentioned he'd been sick. I would love to have seen him one more time.

Dr. Pawan K. Singal

I watched the webcast of the funeral. Memories from his "kids", now adults, were wonderful and heartbreaking. He was remembered as the rock of his family, for his steadfast love of his wife, family, in-laws... pretty much everyone he came into contact with.

His colleagues, particularly my friends Drs. Grant Pierce and Lorrie Kirshenbaum, delineated his achievements, appointments and awards, of which there were many. I was immediately reminded of the time I needed some fancy-looking awards for use in a research centre video. Dr. Singal, by then director of the Institute of Cardiovascular Sciences, allowed me to take the two awards from his office wall. When I said I needed a few more, he told me to look in his lab office. I returned a few minutes later, empty-handed.

"You need to look behind the door on the top two shelves."

And there, piled like cordwood, were at least a dozen plaques, some unopened since he unpacked his bag.

I suppose it is necessary to list one's achievements at one's funeral. Dr. Singal was a world-renowned cardiovascular researcher after all. His work impacted lives worldwide. He was known, worldwide. But physical awards didn't mean as much to him as the relationships that were made through receiving them.

Of course equal due was given his easy demeanour, his physically large stature, his distinct baritone voice, his sense of humour, and his unquestionable love of family... of humanity actually. People loved him, and he loved them.

My career in communications has been in support of biomedical researchers. They are busy people, and I tried not to waste their time in our brief confabs. Often distraction would eventually appear in their eyes and mannerisms, and I would cut the meetings short.

This was never the case with Dr. Singal. He always had time for me. Always smiling, welcoming... he'd often offer me coffee, and always opened with a question about my family.

"So Bill, any plans for the summer? Is Christian playing baseball this year? You'll have to let me know when he starts hockey in the fall. I'd like to come to a game."

I always felt better about myself, felt valued and appreciated, after spending time with Dr. Singal. And I believe I worked all the harder because of it. He motivated me.

THAT's what a real leader does.

His loss will reverberate through the cardiovascular research community for many years to come. I feel his loss professionally, but more so personally. I am proud to have called him my friend.

Paging Dr. R.D. Weinberg

It's a remarkable reversal of roles.

Twenty years ago, when I got home from work my son would always ask "How's yer day?" I loved his inquisitive mind, and how he actually listened when I gave the answer, sometimes making up details to make a mundane day seem interesting. This little exchange would always make my day.

Now I am retired, and wait for Christian to come home from student teaching high school students at Collège Lorette Collegiate. Today I asked him the question, "So, how was your day?" He responded "Good." This was not the deal. The deal is I get a story, as he did 20 years ago. So I pressed on.

"Enlighten any young minds today?"

"I suppose so."

This was like pulling teeth. "What were you teaching?"

"Biology. Hardy-Weinberg."

I pretended to know what he was talking about. While he poked around on his phone, I casually pretended to do the same. It took some time; I started trying to Google "R.D. Weinberg" as that's what I heard. Nothing. Then, "biology and Weinberg" turned up the Hardy-Weinberg Principle.

"...also known as the Hardy-Weinberg equilibrium, model, theorem, or law, states that allele and genotype frequencies in a population

will remain constant from generation to generation in the absence of other evolutionary influences."

Yeah, uh, ok.

A little further reading gave me some insight; the article further listed the influences – including genetic drift, mate choice, assortative mating, natural selection, sexual selection, mutation, gene flow, meiotic drive, genetic hitchhiking, population bottleneck, founder effect, inbreeding and outbreeding depression.

Wait. Inbreeding? That one caught my attention, and gave me the ammunition I was looking for.

"So, did you cover inbreeding?" I provoked. He didn't even look up from his phone.

"I'm covering that tomorrow."

Father's Day, 2023

I received the most interesting card from the kids today. Well, truth be told it was written by Christian (in his handwriting anyway) and presumably edited or at least approved by Olivia, as she was away at that moment. It is beautifully written, and includes all the sentiments that fathers should receive from their children. I will spare the details, except for this... it contains the words (I am not making this up) "venturous", "circumspect", and "moreover".

How time has flown by.

The card is currently displayed on the mantle. Then, per tradition, it will mysteriously disappear into the memory box in my closet, where pretty much every card I have ever received from them is stored. I'm a bit of a memorabilia hoarder in this way.

Back when they were youngsters, the Father's Day messages were so much less formal. I found an old one, also from the both of them, where the following was handwritten:

"Dear Dad, I love that you give me hugs and kissis." – Olivia

"Dear Dad, I love that you take me outside." – Christian

The latter message was transcribed by Roula, hence the perfect spelling. I am certain she coordinated the creation of the gigantic card by simply asking them what they loved about me. Their answers perfectly reflected the times, and made my heart swell. Still does.

Today's card did as well, though written in the vernacular of the two university graduates they've become. No less sweet, but man how time has passed!

And for the record, I am still perfectly willing to give Olivia hugs and "kissis" when needed, and Christian and I just got back from a week-long motorcycle trip to the Black Hills, so I guess I'm still taking him outside...

Chips and dip

The Peters family is renowned for consuming copious quantities of ripple chips and dip (dry French onion soup mixed with sour cream) at every family gathering. There are no leftovers. Ever. Even the dip bowl is cleaned by mixing in chip dust and using a spoon. All of those who've dared to marry into the clan know this, and have chips at the ready if there's even a chance of hosting a gathering.

As of Christmas 2023 and on doctor's orders, I have drastically reduced the fat and salt content in my diet. And sadly this now includes chips.

Some eight months later and with considerable exercise, I have near normalized my blood pressure, and lost over 20 lbs. This accomplishment has garnered the praise and adoration of my siblings!

Just kidding about that last part.

Now I write Haiku about chips instead...

Potato goodness

With essential onion dip

Ripple is the best.

Everything I needed to know

It has been 57 years since I started Grade 1 at Minnetonka School. I've said that my first real crush was on the teacher, Miss Unger. I don't really think about her or the school much, except in my writings, but I drove by the school the other day, and saw a light on in the Grade 1 window. And a few days later, last night, I had this dream...

I'm attending a reunion; not of the elementary part of the school, but the junior high which I attended for a year and a half. It's not a reunion of a specific year, rather of all years, so there are hundreds of former students attending. The school has been meticulously cleaned for the occasion, and there are many students moving about the hallways that I don't recognize, who share the common Minnetonka experience.

I am with three others my age, but they are not identified in the dream. I tell them that I'd like to explore the long hall of the elementary section, and they accompany me. Students are milling about, gathering in clusters, laughing and sharing memories. I see the multipurpose room that we used as a gym, the office of Principal Wally Stoyko, the janitorial room where we cleaned the chalkboard erasers, and the now-decorated doorways from Grade 6 down to the last door of Grade 1. And standing in that doorway with a huge smile and beckoning us to join her is fellow Grade 1 alum Judy Wiegner.

The classroom is full of six-year-old students and the chairs and tables are suitably proportioned, forcing us to sit upright. Every student in the room is smiling at us. "I'm Miss Unger." says the teacher, who although youthful in appearance has aged appropriately. There is an immediate and enthusiastic standing ovation.

Struggling to stand from the tiny chairs, we join the ovation. As I stand I look out over the grade ones and notice their number has increased from thirty to one hundred. Then three hundred. The doorway in which we came is barely visible in the distance, and the grade ones, all standing beside their desks, all clapping and hooting cheers, now number in the thousands. Miss Unger silences them all with a wave of her hand, and they sit in their desks. They are still smiling. Beaming.

Miss Unger directs her attention to me. Between us is a display case, with hundreds of meticulously decorated miniature bottles; each individually crafted with beads, glitter, and hand-drawn pictures. She asks a student to remove one bottle from the case to show me. The student is obviously proud to have been selected, and places a bottle on the counter to show me.

"Every year I give each of my students a clear glass bottle, and ask them to put their full creativity into decorating it as they wish, to reflect their individual personality. Then I give them a small piece of paper on which they write one wish, and we seal it inside."

Miss Unger stands back and looks to see if I understand. The student returns the finely decorated bottle to the cabinet, unopened. I notice all the bottles are sealed with wax, and, other than their unique decoration, none of them are labeled. There are thousands of them, and together their beauty is unimaginable.

Miss Unger looks at me knowingly. I look around the classroom, and now there is no one there except the two of us.

She sees that I don't understand.

"Yes, your bottle is here, but you will never find it, and it will remain unopened. To do so would spoil the beauty of this collection of hopes, wishes, and dreams. You don't remember what you wrote, few of the students do. You are a part of something larger than yourself, yet your contribution is unique, special, and equal to everyone else's.

It was at this point that I woke up.

This kind of dream fascinates me. Can philosophical thought really continue when you sleep?

Changing of the season

Just wait. Soon we'll be enjoying the fresh plus temperature air, watching patches of grass emerge from the snow, carving paths for the snowmelt to make its way to the drains, hearing the birds chirping their return, watching buds bloom. Then hearing your first lawnmower of the season and seeing your neighbours talking on the street.

We get to experience new birth EVERY year! Sure, we are a little tired of the bleakness and mundanity of the season. But, like Christmas in December, summer is coming. And it is the journey as much as the destination that counts!

Don't wish away your life. It's far too short.

Sweet, sweet chili

Me: *How do you like the chili?*

Roula: *It's good! How much sugar did you put in it?*

Me: *I can't remember. Two cups?*

Roula: *Ugh! That's way too much! I don't know if I can eat this anymore! I'm going to have something else. You shouldn't eat this either. Far too much sugar!*

Me (after reading the recipe): *Oops. Two tablespoons.*

Roula: *Next time don't add sugar.*

Into the breach

I bravely, thoughtlessly, jumped into the breach tonight.

Pulled into the driveway, and as I emerged, canvasses and epoxy (new art project) in hand, I noticed two furry, chubby bears bounding across the street toward the neighbour's flower garden. I put my art supplies down, summoned inner courage and walked calmly and purposefully toward them. It was on!

They stopped in their tracks and looked directly at me. One took a couple of steps toward me, its tail wagging furiously. Then they both locked eyes on me, as if... hold on, tail? Bears don't have tails! At least not long ones.

Turns out they were escapees from the next neighbourhood, out enjoying their freedom. I sat on the curb; a woman stood in her living room window, watching. Both dogs approached cautiously; one, "Milo", allowed me to check her collar for ID. A quick call to the number on the tag and I was soon talking with the out-of-breath owner. "Missing your dogs?" I asked.

Within 10 seconds she appeared, phone in hand, at the end of the block. While the other bolted to meet her, Milo stayed with me. And that's how I met a neighbour from the next hood. Lovely woman who still has no idea how they escaped her fenced yard.

Another world

It has become abundantly clear that Roula and I are watching American Political Drama unfold on CNN like it's the soap *Another World*. We catch each other up, there are characters we love and others not so much, there are unbelievable plot twists, most of the male characters are old and distinguished, the women are often stylish and beautiful. And you can watch for months and nothing really progresses much.

The plot line: Over the years, handsome (and single!) newsman Anderson Cooper casually flirts with his guests and is a regular on the talk show circuit. Son of fashion designer Gloria Vanderbilt, herself an heiress to an immense family fortune, he is gay, and through surrogacy now has an incredibly cute son. Currently Anderson is growing increasingly frustrated with the Republican Party, and worries openly that President Trump (a pompous, narcissistic, sexist ex reality TV star who also comes from money) might win a second term.

Trump loses the election (or does he?!) and faces a second (yes second!) impeachment trial...

You get the gist. My point is this soap has had us hooked for several years now, and sustains us through the boredom of retirement and COVID quarantine.

God Bless America!

Just Vince

Olivia called; reason enough to put down my hammer and take a break from the mundane task of pulling crooked nails from a pile of two-by-fours. She immediately let me know that Vince Fontaine had passed away. Good thing I had sat down, I felt light-headed from the shock of the news. Vince and I are the same age.

Vince Fontaine

I had seen Vince only a month ago, December 9th to be exact, sitting with one of his daughters in the Grant Park Mall. I'd been having coffee with my mom, across the cluster of booths by Tim Hortons. I thought to wave them over, but after clearing off the seats beside us I looked up and they were gone.

Some years ago I was introduced to Vince, either by his wife Dorothy, or brother-in-law Steve, I don't recall. I saw him in church occasionally, and he would offer a shy wave or smile, and a "Hi Bill." Our kids knew each other through youth or Sunday school. I might see him at one of Steve's concerts. Always a nod of recognition, and a "Hi Bill."

In the days after Olivia's call, Facebook exploded with tributes to Vince; recognition for his leadership and service to his culture and community, his humble nature despite winning acclaim as a prominent First Nations songwriter and musician. A Go Fund Me in support of his family and costs associated with a celebration of life, planned for Sunday at the Forks' Oodena Celebration Circle. No doubt hundreds will attend, and he will be remembered for all who he was, though he was just Vince to me.

I must admit that, sadly, I never saw Vince play. Never heard him sing. Somehow, our musical paths never crossed. This saddens me now.

But I will remember Vince, mostly because he always made the effort to remember me, by name.

Miigwech, Vince. Chi-miigwech.

Things I learned from my dad

My dad, Mr. Bill Peters Sr.

1. Be early.

2. Stay until the job is done.

3. Your word is your bond.

4. Never be stuck.

5. Put the tools back where you found them.

6. If you don't know how, ask.

7. Get to bed at a decent time.

8. If someone asks you to go for coffee, go.

9. Measure twice, cut once.

10. Be a landlord, not a renter.

11. Make your money work for you.

12. Don't buy things that depreciate with borrowed money.

13. Buy a house as soon as you are able.

14. You can never have too many tools.

15. Earn respect, and pay respect when it is due.

16. There is right, and wrong.

17. If you are not interested in the sermon, review your week and plan the next one.

18. Surround yourself with people you want to be like.

19. Celebrities are people too.

20. Churches take from those who have, to help those who don't. Aim to be in the first category.

21. Learn to say "hello" in as many languages as you can.

22. Education is important. Skills are important too.

23. Buy the best quality you can afford.

24. Be there when your family needs you.

25. Buy a good chainsaw. You can pay for it in two tree jobs.

26. Lincolns are better than Cadillacs.

27. If you want to know how the daughter will turn out, look at her mother.

28. Buy a snowblower, and help people who only have shovels.

29. Buy, rent, repeat.

30. Wash your car.

31. Politicians are popularity contest winners.

32. You can move the world with the right lever.

It's all white now

I heard something funny at Argy's record store today. A young black man brings in some records to sell, and says to owner Ray "Got some old R&B and soul records. And some Caucasian ones too." Ha!

He backpedalled when I called him on it, but we all laughed at what he said. It reminded me of how Roula's family referred to pretty much everyone outside the Greek community as "English". Of course they meant English-speaking, but there was always an Us vs. Them undertone. Makes me think about how visible minorities must come to view the world as "us, and everyone else". Our Pakistani neighbours are a little like that too; when we first moved here I'd ask about their family, food, customs, religious holidays, etc., because I was genuinely interested. They know me well enough now to know that I was just trying to break through what makes us different, and find common ground.

The best part for me is when we can laugh at our ignorance, and move on. And you have to admit, "Caucasian music" is kind of funny. A new category for the Grammys?

Moving the world

In this electronic age, it is hard to find an example of something practical, learned from my father that I could pass on to my son. Then this happened; I needed to move a 1,200 lb. rock across the yard. "You can move the world with a lever." my dad used to say. (see number 32 in the list) And so, with the aid of a hydro cross arm and some rocks for fulcrums, we lifted the rock onto some posts and rolled it, Egyptian-style, into place. He would have been proud!

"Never be stuck." – Bill Peters Sr.

Being there

Another Father's Day has come and gone. It's been years since Dad passed, but he is very much a part of my life and who I am. I still seek his counsel, and find answers to life's challenges as he did – in moments of deep thought just before sleep.

He taught me many things, mostly by example. He fixed things. He didn't waste time. He had a "right or wrong" philosophy. But mostly, he was there for me when I needed him. And he still is.

It wasn't an easy relationship; there were pressures and expectations that came with being the first son. When his expectations were unmet, he openly displayed and verbalized his disappointment. I needed his approval, and find that I still conduct myself in ways I think would earn it. Some of his friends say I look just like him; others say I AM just like him. I guess I am slowly becoming him; a predestination to which I am uncomfortably resigned. Hopefully I will do him justice, and in whatever ways possible – be a little bit better.

God knows we butted heads! I certainly carry his stubbornness gene, and argument characterized most of my teen years. My best moment came in an exasperated response to his goading me into admission that his "negative reinforcement" tactics were, in fact, effective. "You have taught me everything I need to know to be a great father," I said. "What you did well, I will do. And the things you did poorly, I will never do." He got the point, and in the latter years of his life, he came to respect my abilities as a father.

Of course I have made many mistakes, but by the time you think you've perfected your technique, they've grown up and you've lost control. Hopefully the kids know I've done the best I could. And if they strive to be even better at it than I, well, good luck to them. I've done my job. And in that respect I suppose my dad did his.

I received a homemade card from the kids this year, along with an electric screwdriver. "You can never have too many tools", my dad would say. And written in the card...

"Thank you for all your love and support, and for always being there when we need you."

And I always will be. Trust me on that.

Off-Centre

When the St. Boniface Hospital Foundation sold the naming rights to Paul Albrechtsen, they pulled the old lettering "Research Centre" off of the building and laid it out on the floor of the atrium. From there, staff could take a memento. I took the four-foot letter C.

I had plans for it... a bedroom wall decoration for Christian (no thanks, Dad), a solar-powered light for our deck (uh, no, Bill), well how about on the backyard fence (wouldn't that look tacky?)... It ended up relegated to storage in the far corner of the yard.

Yesterday, after several years of moving it around, I decided to sell it on the Facebook group page, "Sunshine Auctions." It went for $12.

About an hour ago, I woke from a disturbing dream which was as real and frighteningly detailed as any nightmare I've ever had...

I'd been on holidays from my 30-year job at the Centre. Upon my return I found they'd changed the Cohen Auditorium into a hybrid auditorium/Radio Shack, replete with racks of record players and cheap stereos. It was still a functional auditorium, so customers had to squint at the retail products and talk in hushed tones. I was mortified.

I stormed up to the admin office to register my disdain, finding it had been converted to "Tandy Church", Tandy being the parent company of Radio Shack. I was met at the door by the Research Director, and a cadre of suits and dresses that were Hospital Foundation officials. Their director had apparently been dismissed, and was replaced by a finely-coiffed man from Tandy Corp with the appearance and demeanour of a southern Baptist minister. Tandy Corp was fully in charge, and would determine the direction of the Centre from here on in. My incredulity was met with righteous indignation, and though I screamed and fought for the scientific independence of the Centre, well, the decision had been made. I had no choice; the Centre was moving in this direction without me, and though I was emotionally unprepared, resignation was my only choice. I was devastated. The director apologetically walked me out.

* * *

It's 6:37 a.m., and I am glad I sold the letter. And although I have made many cherished friendships at the Centre, it is one more way, a physical manifestation, of doing what's necessary... letting go.

"Whale hump"

Roula: *Did he buy the whale hump?*

Me: *What?*

Roula: *On American Pickers. Did he end up buying the whale hump?*

Me: *A "whale hump"? There was no whale hump!*

Roula (adjusts night guard): *OIL PUMP!*

Me: *Oh. Yes. Good night.*

Thoughts at -35°C

Mailed a letter last night. Had flashbacks to the old days; crisp fresh air in the lungs felt awesome. Today the sun shines brightly, and longer than yesterday. Birds are using my birdhouses. I can build a fire and enjoy it anytime I want. My friends are always home when I call, and actually enjoy talking to me. I can do projects in the garage, play drums in the basement, or take a nap anytime I want! And I can do all of this without even putting my pants on. Life is short, fellas. Enjoy it while you can!

To everything a season

The days shorten. Wind rustles through the leaves. Crisp morning air. The redolent harvest. Pumpkin spice.

The weather turns, and we look to the sky knowing inevitable change is coming. Frost. Then the gently descending flakes – tiny harbingers of winter. Like crystalline paratroopers, they melt into the warm earth. North winds then prevail and the hill is gradually, inexorably captured.

We deny this intrusion, and pound the steering wheel in suddenly congested traffic. We pray for an extension. Our collective mood matches the greying sky. The snowblower exchanges places with the lawnmower in the shed, and before you know it...

Winter is here.

As a kid I embraced this, pulling out the skates, hanging my parka in the front closet; *Hockey Night in Canada's* theme a fanfare simultaneously announcing the passage of summer and the arrival of the season. Béliveau incarnate, I'd slide a puck between two blocks of snow six feet apart, and raise my stick in victory under the ersatz spotlight atop the hydro pole. Layered sweaters under a parka, hand-knit mitts, long johns under well-worn jeans, felt-lined snow boots, topped with a frost-rimmed balaclava... this was the uniform of winter. Achieving equilibrium with the elements was a victory never fully achieved; one could sweat and get frostbite at the same time. And though our complaints were as bitter as the cold, we'd be outside at every opportunity.

Some nights, the neighbourhood kids would pile into a car, toboggan strapped to the roof, and head to St. Vital Park and the wooden slide towers. Banked to the river with the twists and turns of a bobsled run, they were a balance of fun and danger totally unmatched by the international award-winning and mandated safe present-day replacement. Now grandparents wait in the electrically-heated shelter and shake their heads, recalling the smell of burnt polyester mittens on a potbelly wood stove and going home with a purple shiner, proudly displayed as a trophy at school the next day.

Floyd, Karen, and Earl

Last night I invited some of my high school friends to gather around a fire in that same park. Three showed up despite the -26° temperature, and we reminisced for a couple of hours. A remarkable connectedness still exists. The less hardy (perhaps the smarter) will join us again when summer comes, but for that moment we dug in and accepted the harsh challenge of the season.

Later that evening I stood at the kitchen window and surveyed the landscape of my back yard, where I'd built many rinks over the years. Now, there is a circular patio with a fire pit, a deck, and a few raised planters – all covered in a blanket of snow. I found myself planning a retaining wall, a rock garden, and maybe a water fountain.

Winnipeg's climate demands the ability to adapt and change. Each season has inherent beauty, and one just has to go outside and experience it. Accept what you can't change, and change what you can, as they say.

Soon the days will lengthen, the rains will wash away the grit of winter, and the wonders of spring will emerge. Buds will sprout and Canada Geese will return to start their families. Cottages will open, and the "May Long" will signal the arrival of summer.

Inevitable change is coming, so prepare to put away the coats and boots and adapt as you always do. And just as the change of season tightens wood grain, you'll be the stronger for it.

Getting my hands dirty

This is a picture of my hands. They're dirty from wrestling an old tire off of a wheelbarrow.

But when I looked at them today I saw a myriad of things. I saw myself as a young boy loading tree branches on the truck. In the rain, pounding out rusty, bent nails from boards that would be burned, and the nails thrown away (a "make-work" project given by my dad). I saw myself repacking a wheel bearing with grease, sharpening a lawnmower blade, sorting nuts and bolts, putting the tools away. Hauling things, burning things, fixing things. Things I generally hated doing.

I went from the penultimate dirty job on the kill floor at Canada Packers to Red River College, to study journalism and get a "clean" job so I could, in my mind, work smart instead of hard. Use my head instead of my hands. Get a desk job, and be the first male in the Peters family to do so – a major step in the evolution of the Peters family males. What followed college was a successful 37-year career, more or less behind a desk.

When I retired I imagined myself doing choice freelance projects; writing a book, producing a documentary, shooting stock video or photography. I imagined using my talents to their full advantage in this new found freedom.

Not so much.

This morning I am prying a stubborn tire off of a rusty wheelbarrow wheel, using the tools I inherited from my dad. And when I looked at my hands, I saw what my dad gave me.

I can write. I can shoot pictures. I have been offered opportunities to produce video, but retirement should be for doing what you enjoy. And for some reason I now enjoy what I despised as a boy – doing hard work with my hands.

Oh chute

Self-declared Flat Earth researcher and DIY rocketeer "Mad" Mike Hughes died recently when his homemade rocket malfunctioned and crashed.

Although unable to obtain evidence that the earth is flat, he did conclusively prove that it is, in fact, extremely hard.

Godspeed Neil Peart

A few months ago, Christian and I were playing electronic drums, side by side, at Long & McQuade. He started first, with his earphones in. I recognized the pattern and joined in. Customers watched our synchronized playing and smiled at my playing along even though I couldn't hear the music.

I didn't need to; I'd heard it so many times from upstairs, while Christian learned all the intricacies of Rush's *Tom Sawyer*.

Godspeed Neil Peart. Say hi to Buddy Rich for me.

Uptown funk

So I am in Long & McQuade the other day, and as usual I go check out the electronic drums. They have a $6,500 Roland kit, and I can't resist. The headphones are sitting on the snare, so I put them on, pick up the sticks and tap on the snare, which results in the warmest, wettest, resonant crack of sound ever. I glance to the sound module, which displays the words "Funk/Auditorium", hence the resonant sounds. So I close my eyes and play the funkiest groove ever. I'm in the zone. Nobody else is around; not even the enthusiastic clacking outside my headphones would be heard outside the department. Drummer Heaven!

I open my eyes. Still no one in the drum section, but there were five people in various parts of the store that were standing squarely facing me. One staff member smiled and waved as he went into the back room. Others returned to shopping.

So I take the headphones off and place them carefully back on the snare, and the sticks back on the floor tom. But as I do so, a stick drops from my hand and a resounding THUD fills the room.

Apparently the kit was wired live to their PA system.

No good deed

This is not intended to vilify the police or RCMP, in fact I have the utmost respect for them, and the officer that gave me the ticket.

I was charged with violating 61(2) of the *Highway Traffic Act,* for operating a vehicle with an unsecured load:

"No person shall operate, or permit to be operated, upon a highway any motor vehicle or trailer unless the load that the motor vehicle or trailer is carrying is firmly bound, sufficiently covered, or otherwise secured or loaded, in such a manner that no portion of the load may become dislodged or fall from the motor vehicle or trailer."

As 61(2) allows for a load which was "otherwise secured or loaded, in such a manner that no portion of the load may become dislodged or fall from the motor vehicle or trailer." I believe I have a case, although the furor that has transpired over the last few days may end up with these tickets being torn up anyway. At least that is what I, and many others, hope.

The recent snowstorm has rendered the City of Winnipeg incapable of dealing on its own with the huge volume of fallen trees. They have called in reinforcements from neighbouring provinces. And they have implored their citizens to help out where they can.

An elderly neighbour lady's trees took a big hit. Several large apple tree branches broke off and were blocking the sidewalk the Kindergarten to Grade 7 children use to get to the school next door. Some branches were hanging dangerously overhead. I borrowed a truck, then cut and cleared the branches for her, as she was told the city may not get to it for months. It took two trips to the Brady Road landfill. On the second trip I (actually "we", thanks Earl) stomped down the branches and secured the load with a 150 lb. tree limb. I tied a flag on the end of this 9-foot limb as per local regulations. Nothing moved all the way to the dump.

Literally hundreds of Winnipeggers are doing the same thing, as evidenced by the constant flow of half-tons and cars with trailers to the landfill, after an estimated hundred thousand plus trees were damaged or destroyed.

But today, on Brady Road, there sat a Provincial officer handing out tickets to people with "unsecured" loads — one after the other after the other. To people who were only trying to get this work done before the next snowfall. And to people like me who had access to a truck, and time to lend a hand.

I suppose I should have known better, but when the officer pointed to a rickety trailer with an exposed load only barely held down by a thin bungee cord, and said "You'd have avoided this ticket if you had secured your load like that," I nearly lost it. Despite his words, I fully kept my composure. Then he gave me a $300 ticket.

As my brother-in-law said when I returned his truck "I guess good deeds really don't go unpunished."

Lorne Robb, the "legend of Churchill"

Albert Laurence Robb was born on January 22, 1933, one of a set of twins born to Mary Agnes and William Roy Robb, of Dropmore, Manitoba. Predeceased by his parents, his twin brother Clarence, his brother Alvin and sister Kay, he is survived by his youngest sister Irene. Irene is my mother.

He never liked the name Albert, and the childlike cadence of Laurence and Clarence eventually gave way to "Lorne". As a kid I called him

Uncle Laurence; in recent years Uncle Lorne. In speaking with his doctors, nurses, pharmacist, and others over the past year, I've said "His legal name is Albert Laurence Robb, but he goes by Lorne". The nurses at Victoria Hospital wrote "Lorne" on his chart, and you could see he appreciated the familiarity, and informality, that represented. Lorne passed away on May 12, 2019 at the age of 86.

Lorne was an accomplished accounting professional, with impressive careers in banking and as Financial/Administrative Officer for the Town and Port of Churchill. He was active in his communities in sports and fundraising — specifically with the Fort Prince of Wales Masonic Lodge. He "retired" in 1991, and moved to Winnipeg several years later; joining the Commissionaires and providing security services to the Canadian Grain Commission and the Canadian Air Forces Base 17 Wing, among others. And though he'd spent most of his professional life away from family in places as diverse as Kingston, Jamaica; Port William, Ontario; and Churchill, Manitoba, he became a welcomed member of the Peters family. He attended Christmas and Easter events and birthday parties. And although he'd engage in polite conversation, most often he'd find a chair and just listen to the loud banter of the extended Peters family from a distance.

We celebrated with him on his 80th birthday with dinner at the Spaghetti Factory, and he treasured our gift of a Winnipeg Jets sweater.

He lived alone; a "confirmed bachelor" as they say, and had done so as long as I can remember. His visits to Winnipeg were infrequent, and both my sister Bonnie and I thought of him as a swinging bachelor, with charm along the lines of a young Pierre Elliott Trudeau.

I got to know him a little better in the summer of 1975, when he found work for me at a garage in Churchill. The six weeks I spent there was in high contrast to life at home. I wondered how he could live for so long in such a place. But I could see that he kept very busy;

he owned Hudson Motors and was town administrator. He left me alone for the last week to go on a business trip to Ottawa, and I had never felt so isolated, so removed from society. I was so glad to return home; he remained in Churchill through to his retirement in 1991.

After suffering a stroke three years ago, and with illness slowing him down, I convinced Lorne to sell his car and rely on me for rides to the doctor, and grocery shopping. I would see him once a month or so. But as his needs increased, those monthly visits became weekly, then daily, and sometimes two or three times in one day. I saw him at his most vulnerable, but his only complaint is that he felt he was being, in his words, a "pest". But we had become pretty close at that point, and I learned a lot about his character through the process. He was resilient. He was determined. Most of all, he was frustrated. As was I when trying to help him navigate the healthcare system through his final days.

For the past week I have been reflecting on his life, and what I perceived to be his comparative loneliness. I thought of his Churchill years, and actually found a Facebook group, a community billboard of sorts, to which I posted the sad news of his death. Within two days the post was flooded with over 40 messages of sympathy, with personal stories of his friendliness and service to the community. The descriptions included "kind soul", "the whole town knew him", and "he was a legend in Churchill". So maybe he hadn't led such a lonely life after all! I even found out that he'd volunteered in the mid-60s at Churchill's first and fledgling TV station — hosting live music shows and even playing "Uncle Lorne" on a children's TV show! How could we not know?!

Lorne was a humble man, but he accomplished much in his life. And in his prime he was unstoppable. He kept many awards of achievement and citizenship, but he did not display them — I only found them while packing up his apartment this past week. Perhaps most telling of his accomplishments was his membership in the

Fort Prince of Wales Masonic Lodge, where he ascended to the highest rank of Master Mason. I donated a box of certificates and ceremonial paraphernalia to the Masonic Lodge in Winnipeg this week, to which their archivist replied "Your uncle would have been considered very highly in the organization, like a CEO." And after a fairly lengthy chat about Lorne's life in Churchill, he said. "Your uncle may have lived alone, but I can guarantee you he wasn't lonely. He had many brothers."

On my last visit with Lorne, the day before he passed, he was alert and animated, but could not muster the breath to speak. He tried to express something, but just shrugged his shoulders and rolled his eyes in frustration at being unable to do so. I am sure he was trying to say that he knew he was dying, and that it would be OK. He waved goodbye as we left, with a slight smile on his face.

Goodbye Uncle Lorne. You will be missed, and fondly remembered by many.

Thoughts and prayers

It's happened again, nothing left to lose.
How many have to die to make the evening news?

Nice young man, self-obsessed.
Loved his mom, who'd have guessed?

Expressions of anguish and pain.
Our hearts go out, again and again.
Emotional burdens can break the back of the strongest man, and instead of sharing the load we offer Thoughts and Prayers.

Thoughts and Prayers. When they need to believe somebody cares.
Thoughts and Prayers.

The only comfort we can give, while children die and killers
live, are
Thoughts and Prayers.

Expressions of anguish and pain.
Hearts are broken again and again and again.
Emotional burdens can break the back of the strongest man, and instead of sharing the load we offer...

Thoughts and Prayers.

The magic of Auntie Kay

Kathleen Isabel Robb, or "Kay" to all of us here, was born June 28, 1925 and passed away on May 24, 2007 just a month short of her 82nd birthday. Kay was predeceased by husband Steve Pomeranski; mother and father Mary and William Roy Robb; and brothers, Alvin and Clarence. She will be greatly missed by her sister Irene (Bill) Peters; brother Laurence Robb; nine nieces and nephews, including Bonnie (Doug) Jerlo, Bill (Roula) Peters, Bob (Karen) Peters, Diane (Harold) Funk, Denise (Scott) Patterson, Bill (Kathy) Robb,

Karen Robb, Debbie Robb, and Scott Pomer — and our combined 14 children — all of whom had tremendous and unconditional love from their Auntie Kay.

Kay spent her childhood in Dropmore, Manitoba, and enjoyed sports — especially curling and baseball. Church was an important part of Robb family life, and Kay played the piano at most of the services, which were held in the community hall. She found work as a teen in Winnipeg, but returned to Dropmore to help with her ailing mom. Returning to Winnipeg in 1955, Kay worked at a grocery store, and after her mother's passing in 1958 took care of her father until his passing in 1973. Then after three years she found her life partner in Steve Pomeranski, and they were together for 17 years until his passing in 1993.

After some time alone she then began to enjoy high-rise apartment living in downtown Winnipeg — her apartments having a wonderful view of the Forks Market. She still loved her sports, and would watch curling, baseball, and football especially if the Bombers were playing. Thankfully, Kay had many good friends in her life, and we know she will be missed by them all — particularly the High-Risers, members of Club 22, and Heather, who provided home care and was a good friend.

Kay gave so much time and love to her family, and her hugs and pleasant conversation will be missed more than she could ever know. Her love, generosity and genuine concern for her brothers and sister, nieces and nephews and their children is her legacy — she loved us as her own, and told us so.

My memories of Auntie Kay begin in the mid-1960s, when I was somewhere around six or eight years old. Kay had been taking care of my grandfather after my grandmother's death in 1959, and our family, then three kids and my mom and dad, would go over for supper almost every Sunday. Those memories evoke a kind of "situation comedy" memory for me, with Mom watching over baby Bob, Dad in conversation with Grandpa Robb, with me wreaking havoc at every possible opportunity, while Bonnie kept Mom and Kay informed of my activities. Auntie Kay was our red-haired "Hazel"; preparing dinner while in conversation with Mom, and as much as possible, keeping the little ones out of trouble.

They had an interesting stove in that house — one that with today's safety standards could not exist. It had front-mounted dials that would light up in different colours as they were turned up, from green, to yellow, to bright red. I liked red. Often I would "decorate" the front of the stove with all three colours. I was warned, many times, that this activity was dangerous. So also was playing with the electric kettle, which Kay stored safely out of my reach — on one of the rear elements on the stove. I think she found a safer place for it after I made the connection between one of the dials and that rear element. And yet Kay has never raised her voice to me — her only concern being my safety and well-being.

Kay recently retold a story from those days of my brother Bob, who had provoked some kind of trouble and had been sent to a bedroom upstairs. Sometime later Kay found him sobbing face down on the bed, and when she asked him what the matter was, he told her "Nobody loves me, Auntie Kay." She said to him, "Well I do, Bob." And immediately that made him feel better. As Bob is technically the middle child of our family, Kay always wanted to make sure he felt loved. And we could see that concern for him every time she has told that story through the years.

Over the years, from Thanksgiving and Easter to Christmas, every special family occasion was made more special with the inclusion of Auntie Kay. The food was always great, and the mood lighter. And I would be remiss not to mention that she had a wonderful sense of humour!

Many years have passed since those early memories, and with time came physical problems — first with her knees, then a stroke, then her hip started giving her trouble. And yet every time we visited her she apologized for not being able to make coffee, or serve us in some way. And if she was in pain she would tell us, but would not let it affect her visit with our kids. And though we knew that she would smoke, she never once smoked when we were there which at times was for an entire evening.

I think her life is best summed up in this way... As a small child and throughout my life I knew I could go to Auntie Kay and receive love and a big hug like I was her favorite son. Every one of us kids could. Only two days ago I asked my 10-year-old son if he felt comfortable coming to Auntie Kay's service and at first he said he'd rather not. When I asked him why, he did not hesitate to say "Because I love Auntie Kay." And it is for that same reason that he, I, and we are here today. You only have to take a look at the colour picture in the center of the collage of today's program to see the magic of Auntie Kay.

God Bless you Auntie Kay, and thanks for the memories.

The ring

Dear Roula,

You know how bad I am with occasion gifts — always getting you the wrong size, or colour, or gift... I never seem to get it right. But that doesn't mean that I have given up trying.

It started with your wedding ring. I wanted to give you something with a unique design, and a large, high-quality diamond. I found out that I couldn't afford both quality and size, and so I opted for quality. We went together to pick out a ring, and you chose the same one I had... maybe with a little prompting from me. Money was tight in those days!

Then our first Christmas; I got you a blue coat that I just thought was perfect for you. You got me cologne. And that was the beginning of a long string of "gift fails" that went on for years. But as I said, *I haven't given up trying.*

Maybe it's the challenge of the season; birthdays, Christmas, Valentines... all come with their unique pressures — both for buying and receiving gifts. Not to mention (mostly unmet) expectations. It would be so easy to throw up my hands and give up. Or give you gift cards. Or cash.

But *I haven't given up trying*. And so this gift, given to you purposely on no particular occasion, is my latest way of saying I love you. Every day.

When I knew that I would be having open heart surgery, even though the survival odds were all in my favour, I decided to work with an artist to create a gift that would tell the story of what brought you to me, and what we have created together since. And since you still have my first gift to you (the ring), I decided another ring would be a safe bet. But this time it's a "statement ring"!

I wanted the ring to reflect your being Greek, and so it "reads" like a story on a Grecian urn. The symbols tell the story if read from one side of the ring to the other. The designs are all inset, and bordered with a raised edge; mirroring the use of filigree inlay in ancient Greek jewelry.

You are represented on the ring by an 8mm ruby, your birthstone. The rest of the ring is your, and our, story…

It starts with Grecian waves which symbolize your journey by ship from Greece to Pier 21 at Halifax. Next to the waves is a small Peridot stone which symbolizes your parents' risk to come to Canada and hope for a better life for their family. You may know that "Peridot" comes from the Greek word "Peridona" which translated means "giving plenty". Following the Peridot are three little shoemaker's nails and a stalk of wheat, representing your life in Brandon.

The top half of the ring symbolizes the life that we have built together. Olivia, Christian and I are represented by the three small rubies next to yours. There are also bitter almonds and honey — representing the Greek wedding we should have had. The bitter almonds and honey are "scattered" along the ring to symbolize loyalty through the sweet times as well as the hard times...

I hope you come to love this ring, and appreciate what it represents — your life journey becoming part of mine, and my eternal and unwavering love for you.

With love as always,
Bill

God Bless the heroes

After the emotional funeral and tributes to Maurice "The Rocket" Richard, and hearing yet another journalist (Peter Mansbridge with Dick Irvin) remark that most people there had not seen Richard play, I want to remind Winnipeggers who may have seen him play as I did — on January 17, 1969 in an old-timers game at Winnipeg Arena.

He was 47, retired only nine years, and was a member of the Montreal NHL Old-timers in a game against the Western Canada Old-timers. I was eight years old, hadn't played organized hockey yet, and this was my first exposure to the old arena and big-time hockey. After, I was in my glory getting autographs from Butch Bouchard, Frank Selke, Gerry McNeil... even Jack Wells!

Though my dad was certainly a Canadiens fan, I know he was not particularly fond of Mr. Richard and his fiery style of play. He preferred Jean Béliveau's gentlemanly conduct, and often encouraged me to make him my hockey hero.

After the game, when in an almost confrontational manner he called out to the Rocket to sign his son's program, I didn't know what to expect. Mr. Richard turned, put his bag and overcoat down, and spoke to my dad while signing my program. What they said I can't recall, as I think I was in some state of embarrassment and shock. I still have that program to this day.

Twenty-six years later I had the opportunity to take my dad to an NHL Old-timers game in which Mr. Richard was honorary referee. This time it was me who yelled to Richard to autograph a book for me. I still have that one too.

God Bless the heroes!

Crazy 'bout a Mercury

I admit I have a romance with cars and trucks.

The romance began with the cool cars my uncles owned, specifically a 1965 Ford Galaxy XL (Uncle Ed), a 1967 Dodge Monaco (Uncle Isaac), and a shiny red 1968 Pontiac Firebird (Uncle Henry). There were trucks too; a 1968 GMC 1/2-ton on which I honed my driving skills (Isaac again), and the 1949 Mercury 1/2-ton truck he had since new. I absolutely loved that truck, and throughout my early teens I imagined the day my uncle would let me drive it.

To be honest, I was kind of obsessed with that truck. By the time I came to love it I was 12 years old and the Merc was 23 and already relegated to the back of the farm. I dreamt he might give it to me on my 16th birthday, complete with the Oldsmobile 350 rocket engine he planned to put in it. But that was my dream and not his; the rocket was eventually repurposed and the motorless Merc sat sadly beside the farm's Quonset for many years, and in 1997 only the top of the truck was visible when the 100-year flood overtook the farm.

As it sat since 1997.

Since then I've always taken the time to check it out when I visited my uncle. I'd ask about it; even grew bolder over the years, telling my uncle that he should sell me the thing so it could see life again. But he always said no, he'd get to it someday and maybe find another engine to put in it. And so it sat and sat, and eventually succumbed to the fate of so many other vehicles on the farm – it was dragged into the bushes and left to rot.

And then one day not too long ago Isaac told me he was selling the farm to move into Niverville, and an auctioneer had been invited to assess the farm assets. He'd been particularly excited about the Mercury as there is quite a demand for them locally. I must admit my heart sank a bit with the thought of someone else restoring the truck and enjoying it as I had planned for so many years. "But I told him it's not available," Isaac said, "I want you to have it, that is, if you still want it."

So for the last few weeks I have been dreaming as I did so many years ago. And I have so been enjoying the experience of reliving those dreams.

But today, when I went to the farm to help my uncle pull the truck out of the trees, I told him that I no longer wanted it. The auctioneer was right, it would be in demand and perhaps more people will come to the auction as a result. And we spent a glorious afternoon, with my 90-year-old uncle finally pulling the old girl into the sunlight – with all four wheels stubbornly locked up the whole way.

I hadn't sat in the cab of a tractor in 30 years…

I will miss the Merc, but there is some solace here. This summer I hope to complete the restoration of another vehicle that has been my dream to own – as now I do my Uncle Henry's 1968 Firebird.

You see I've wanted THAT car since I was eight!

Remembering Constable John Constable

My daughter tells me it wasn't a true random sample.

This evening's episode of *The Good Wife* was particularly entertaining; so much so that when commercials intervened I did not go to the kitchen for a drink or a snack, rather, I decided to wait them out.

A few minutes in and I noticed a distinct pattern of gun usage in the programs being advertised. So when TGW ended I rewound the PVR back to the commercial break and watched them again.

The opening ad was a promo for *Limitless*, with its foreboding fear of death, darkness and loss of control. This, oddly, was followed by a Boston Pizza commercial. No guns, but the obnoxious soccer announcer yelling "GOOOOaaallll!!!" when patrons ate their pizza was off-putting enough.

A few lightweight kitchen cleaner ads, then a promo for *Supergirl*, a lightweight action-adventure program.

And then another for *Limitless*, this time reacting to the fear and loss of control with guns (2). Fighting back, I get that...

The Blacklist is a crime drama with more guns (5). I guess that makes sense; when *"a former U.S. Navy officer turned high-profile criminal, voluntarily surrenders to the FBI after eluding capture for decades"*, well, one needs more guns.

Next was *Chicago*, a *"high octane view into the lives of everyday heroes"*. Apparently hoses are insufficient; no fewer than 12 guns made an appearance in the 30-second commercial. Now that's fighting fire with firepower!

Elementary served as an interlude. No guns, just the usual witty repartee.

Last but not least, the Naval Criminal Investigative Service needed at least 11 guns to get the job done. *NCIS: Los Angeles* is an undercover unit; maybe someone should tell them to conceal their weapons.

Then back to *The Good Wife*. No guns in this episode, but Alicia and Diane did agree that Cary Agos was no Will Gardner. Will was shot and killed in the courtroom back in the fifth season.

Guns play an integral role in defining America, and there has been a marked increase in their use in American TV. Reminds me of a quote by Oscar Wilde:

"Life imitates Art far more than Art imitates Life."

Perhaps there is truth in Oscar's words. The open carry laws recently passed in Texas seem to support this. Gun violence statistics certainly seem to. I guess what I am saying is man, I miss *The Beachcombers!* Constable John Constable had a gun, but I think he only used it to scare off bears.

Testament to a friend, and a stranger

After high school I worked a variety of jobs. First at Goodyear Tire (boss didn't like my work ethic), then Cam Gard Supply (fired for arguing with the boss's secretary) followed by Advance Electronics; all the while playing drums in a new wave band called The Photoz. In the fall of 1979 I left Advance and the band, and started at the University of Winnipeg with the vague intent of becoming a lawyer. Disappointed and disillusioned with my inabilities in Economics and Political Science (I was doing well in Psychology, Sociology and Advanced French) I left to take a job at Hildebrand Music and Jewellery in Steinbach by Christmas. I didn't know that I could simply drop courses; I thought it was all or nothing.

Thus began the journey to find myself.

I don't think I sold anything for the few months I was there, but when one of the Winnipeg stores lost its manager I was promoted to Winnipeg. I learned to do the books and make deposits, but I don't remember making a single sale there either. Not only was I fired, the owner took me to court for theft of a bass guitar. I'd loaned the guitar to a friend of the previous manager and it never found its way back to the store.

Sales were not for me.

In the spring of 1980 I started at Canada Packers as a general labourer. At $7.35/hr., I was making HUGE money as the minimum wage was $3.15. When my friend Cyndi (then attending the University of Illinois) introduced me to her roommate Christine, I flew back and forth to visit. Christine and I became good friends, but there was no "spark" as Cyndi predicted. Besides which, Christine told me she'd never consider moving to Canada. She did eventually come to

Winnipeg with Cyndi for a short vacation, but long enough to fall in love on the first day with my friend Bob. They live in Winnipeg and have been married for more than 25 years... but I digress.

On my visits to the University of Illinois, I was exposed to campus keg party life. At one of those parties, when the beer had been flowing for a time, Christine and Cyndi's friends started to talk about graduation and the life that would follow. I was sandwiched between two guys discussing where they hoped to article and eventually practise law. Others had plans to work towards a master's degree; maybe a PhD... And the more they went on, the more claustrophobic I felt, until I had to leave.

Back home, I told my parents little about my trip. All I could think is that I was set to become a failure; in two years my new friends would be graduating from university, getting married, starting families... and I had no idea where I would be or what I would be doing. I went out the front door and ran until I was out of breath. I sat at the side of the road with tears in my eyes.

I suppose being alone with your thoughts can be a good thing, but for me it was torture. I literally had no idea what to aspire to, or what I could become. By the end of my second month at Packers I decided I *had* to go back to school. I made an appointment with my high school counsellor, thinking this was the obvious place to start. I was devastated when he didn't remember me, and pointed me to a stack of brochures. He asked me what I was interested in. I didn't know!

Towards the end of the three-month probationary period at Packers I was shuffled through several departments, and on the final day found myself packing pork hocks into boxes. It was tedious, mind-numbing work. The elderly man who trained me didn't mind; he chatted with various people in the department and had a broad smile. I thought maybe he had plans for the weekend; turns out it was his last day and he was retiring. He knew it was the last day of my probation, and asked what my plans for the future were.

A week or so earlier I had run into a school friend who was completing her studies at Red River College. She asked me what I'd been up to, and when I told her about my job she asked me if I'd ever heard about the Creative Communications program. "It's what you've always been good at" she said. And so I applied, as did 200 others. And despite the fact I'd never published anything, and was working as a meat packer, I was accepted.

When the elderly man asked me about my plans for the future, I told him that I was saving to go back to school.

"That's what I said when I started here" he replied, *"30 years ago."*

It's been over 30 years since then, and I now realize that I had run into two of the two most influential people in my career that week; Cheryl Liessens, who had noticed what I was good at, and a retiring Canada Packers worker who inadvertently gave me the resolve to complete my education in creative communications.

It's been a long and fruitful journey. Eternal thanks to both of you.

I retired as Manager of Communications and Media Services at St. Boniface Hospital in Winnipeg, Canada, where my work has gained national and international recognition. For what it's worth, I was named Communicator of the Year by the Canadian Public Relations Association (Manitoba) in 2013.

Essay: American Hitler

(Written before Trump became President the first time)

An article published in the *Journal of Communication,* "Television News and the Cultivation of Fear of Crime" postulates that, despite declining trends in crime, widespread fear of crime in the USA is fueled by heavy exposure to violent TV programming, both news and movies.

This should not surprise.

In my 56 years I've seen a proliferation of American "Us vs. Them" movies. It seems that the US of A needs to have an enemy at the ready to have a sense of self/purpose; whether it be Germany (hundreds of WWII movies); Russia (*Dr. Strangelove, A Good Day to Die Hard*); Iran (*Argo, On Wings of Eagles*); or maybe even China (though while in post-production for *Red Dawn* the invading army was changed from Chinese to North Korean in order to maintain access to China's box office. Maybe they're not quite ready to take them on...)

In the first *Die Hard* movie, Bruce Willis' character John McClane is characterized by German villain Hans Gruber as "just another American who thinks he's John Wayne". McClane, through several sequels, is consistently played as an aggressive, foul-mouthed, wisecracking, no-nonsense, never-say-die, maverick vigilante, who ultimately triumphs as a reluctant hero. And even though the aforementioned *A Good Day to Die Hard* was panned by many critics, Americans ate it up and it grossed over $300 million. Take that, comrades!

Authoritarianism and the politics of fear

Matthew MacWilliams, who carries a PhD in American Politics, recently wrote about the propensity for authoritarianism, specifically defined as

Americans' inclination to authoritarian behaviour. *"People who score high on the authoritarian scale value conformity and order, protect social norms, and are wary of outsiders. And when authoritarians feel threatened, they support aggressive leaders and policies."*

Enter Donald Trump direct from TV land, vilifying Mexicans, Muslims, Women, (even us Canadians) with McClane-esque foul-mouthed recklessness:

"They (Muslims) are not coming to this country if I am president."

"I will build a great wall — and nobody builds walls better than me, believe me — and I'll build them very inexpensively. I will build a great, great wall on our southern border, and I will make Mexico pay for that wall. Mark my words."

"The only kind of people I want counting my money are little short guys that wear yamakas every day."

"You know, it really doesn't matter what the media write as long as you've got a young and beautiful piece of ass."

"It is not the truth that matters, but victory."

Oops, my bad. That last one was a quote from Adolph Hitler.

If Americans followed international news (or even cared about other nations' opinions) they'd know that the world is watching. And they are either laughing or they are concerned that Americans have gone crazy and Trump could actually win.

Be careful what you wish for, America.

Lunch with POTUS

March 17, 2005
To: president@whitehouse.gov
Subject: One President to Another

Dear President Bush,

I must start this email with a story, inspired by my eight-year-old son.

An announcement appeared one morning in the *Winnipeg Free Press,* relating the news of my election as President-Elect of the Health and Science Communications Association. I left the paper open to that story and went upstairs to shower for work. Upon my return, my son Christian was having breakfast at the table. He looked up from the paper and said "Dad, you should have lunch with the President." I asked him what he meant. He then said to me "I know you are important, because I read in the paper that you are going to be President. President Bush is a president too — you should have lunch with him and talk." I started to explain why that would be near impossible, but thought it would be a better lesson to Christian to tell him that I would at least make the offer.

And so... I am offering to buy you lunch. The time/place doesn't matter as I would obviously make myself available at your convenience. Having said that, I will be in DC for our annual International Conference on Healthcare Communication in June of 2006, and I would be happy to see you then!

I await your reply. In June of this year I will take the reins as president of HeSCA. I hope my term of office will aid in some small way in giving our two great nations one more thing in common.

Best regards,

Bill Peters
President-Elect
Health and Science Communications Association

I waited patiently for a reply... nothing came.

And so the following June off I went, family in tow, to Washington DC. And after a successful meeting we decided to stay another week to see the sights. And visit the White House. And though I didn't end up having lunch with the President...

I am pretty sure he knew I was there!

George and me

Darkness over a city of light

Of course I read and heard of the terrorist attacks in Paris.

Memories flooded back of news of the 9/11 attacks on the car radio as I was dropping Christian off at preschool. It was surreal how, on the subsequent drive to work, other drivers appeared like drones — obviously focused on the news from every radio station. No animation on anyone's face, just dogged determination to get to work. Televised news played on the foyer monitor all day; no work was done. I went home and stood in the driveway as everyone went into the house. The sky was silent. The newscasts continued well into the night, each echoing the refrain of the others — what's next?

After the kids went to bed, Roula and I asked each other the same question. I had no answers. Only tears, and a cloud of depression that has come and gone ever since – and returned with the latest news.

This morning I took advantage of a beautiful sunny fall morning to walk to Petro-Can for the weekend paper, which was emblazoned with the headline "Darkness over City of Light". I paid, tucked the paper under my arm, and said thanks to the polite young East Indian man at the counter. He wished me a good day as I left. On the way home I passed a couple of new neighbours, both Asian; a middle-aged couple who said "Good morning", then a young girl who said "Hey" and her mother who smiled and nodded. Another neighbour drove by and waved.

When I walked into the house, Roula had a CD playing while she started doing the weekend laundry. The song, *Violence* by Jordan St. Cyr, was just ending with this chorus:

We're living in a world of violence
And our hearts bear these scars
Prey unto this cold, harsh environment
That sometimes steals our breath
But this hope that we have will never die

Jordan is the son of Janice and Gerry St. Cyr. I went to high school with Janice and I count both among my friends. They have raised a wonderful family, and Jordan amazes and inspires me.

The cloud of depression is slowly lifting, thanks to my neighbours, this sunny day, and the words from the next generation.

He's right. Hope is what we have.

"Neither shall they learn war..."

Isaiah 2:4... "He shall judge between the nations, and shall decide disputes for many peoples; and they shall beat their swords into plowshares, and their spears into pruning hooks; nation shall not lift up sword against nation, neither shall they learn war anymore."

Many years ago my Mennonite ancestors were forced to choose between giving up a tenet of their faith (non-participation in military service) and uprooting their families and moving to a new land. They were an oppressed people; they knew they would endure hardship beyond comprehension, so they set off for the unknown. They had hope for a better future.

They left behind a prosperous farm life and family in order to do this. Their children would be born Canadian, and would endure hardship so that their children's children would have the possibility of a great life. It was a gamble, but they did what they felt they had to do.

I am one of the many descendants who have benefited from their hardship.

I've often wondered what it would be like to go back and look into the faces of the descendants of those who stayed. No doubt they would think and act quite differently from me, but I think the familial similarities would win the day and we'd connect somehow.

The succeeding generations slowly assimilated into Canada. Some of them served in the military. Some farmed, and some became involved in the Canadian political system. Most saw the ideals of this peacekeeping nation as congruent with their pacifist culture. Most remained until this day. Most, but not all.

Some branches of the family looked for greener pastures south of the border. Brothers separated from brothers, sisters from sisters. And in my case, cousins from cousins. At first, frequent visits back and forth kept us in touch. But over the years we eventually lost touch — with the exception of funerals and the odd wedding, we rarely communicated.

With the advent of Facebook, a new avenue of communication opened. For me it has been a wonderful opportunity to reconnect. However, although we are still family, recent world religious and political events have brought forth evidence of the deepening chasm between us – a pro-gun, anti-Muslim philosophy. As one cousin put it:

"... with the anti-Muslim hysteria that prevails in the USA now-a-days...perhaps we Canadians would feel or react differently if there was an attack of that magnitude (9/11) on our soil....turning the other cheek does not seem to be a popular viewpoint these days".

I had to think about this for a bit... I like to think of myself as capable of independent thought, and yet I am a pacifist in what is generally thought of as a peacekeeping, multicultural country. What if my parents had moved to the USA? Would I think the same way as my American cousins?

I'd like to think not, but I honestly don't know. And now I am considering "unfriending" a cousin because I find his viewpoints unsettling, if not disturbing.

Perhaps this is all moot. At some point, perhaps in my children's generation, our family will have no reason to write and share stories with their American second cousins. The chasm will be too wide and interests parochial.

But I like to think that one day, perhaps while on vacation, my kids will see true familiarity in the eyes of a stranger. And they'd connect somehow.

A word from the fence

I am ignorant, at least in the *Merriam-Webster* dictionary definition of the word, on the topics of atheism and evolution. That is to say, I am "lacking knowledge or information."

Frankly, I am comfortable with that. Many are not.

Atheists provoke, generalizing the religious as invisible magic sky wizard worshipping sheep. They claim science debunks the myth of God. "Ours is not opinion, it's evidence-based fact." Their most vocal leader is Richard Dawkins, whose mission in life is to advance science — and secularism.

And the religious counter, based on what they were taught as youngsters, or experienced as adults. Often the most zealous experienced some kind of life trauma that drew them closer to their God. Those who are educated in their religion are relatively few and remarkably publicity-shy; unfortunately their disciples' ripostes are usually time-worn phrases that will never satisfy the scientist.

And so the arguments continue ad nauseam.

As a child I sang "Jesus loves me, this I know — for the Bible tells me so", and read *"For God so loved the world that he gave his only son, that whosoever believeth in Him shall not perish, but have eternal life"* from the Bible. I was content with that. I have sat through hours upon hours of sermons, often daydreaming about what I'd done the previous week, or what I planned to accomplish the next. I'd heard what I needed to hear.

Similarly, I studied evolution in grade school, where the "Man evolved from apes" line always prompted giggles from the girls, as the boys danced and scratched their armpits. There was your hard evidence! And always mention of the missing link; a kind of escape hatch for the religion we all kept hidden. OK, we're good. On to recess!

Now I am trying to live my life peacefully. Blissfully even.

To my mind, cosmic forces causing stars to evolve over billions of years into beings with cognitive awareness is every bit as fantastic as faith in intelligent design.

So, kudos to both sides. And next time you argue, remember the science of mathematics; the fraction of "knowledge or information" you are employing in your argument is as infinitely small as the universe is large.

And provoking people on their beliefs is just rude.

Father's Day

It is my first Father's Day without him.

The last few have been awkward; he being incapacitated by the stroke. It has been a long time since we had a meaningful conversation and those often seemed one-sided — we being stubborn and opinionated. I miss the garage sales, the odd times when I could make him laugh, or when he'd show he was proud of me. The kids are hard and irrefutable evidence of that.

Strangely, I think of him most when I accomplish something, or when the kids do.

Mom and I are going to the cemetery this afternoon; I am certain Dad would appreciate that. Happy Father's Day, Dad.

Seconds of terror

My first thought was "Oh my God, it's happened".

I woke to CBC morning news on the clock radio at 6:00 a.m. A Lufthansa flight carrying 144 passengers had just crashed in the French Alps, and there were no survivors. My son and dozens of his Westgate Collegiate friends had left from Winnipeg the day before and, at that moment, were on a connecting flight from Frankfurt, Germany to their destination of Amman, Jordan.

Their Middle East school trip had been planned for some time; Christian had been working at IKEA for over a year to save money to pay for the trip himself. He and about 40 others were really looking forward to reuniting with the kids from Mar Elias school in Israel, who visited Winnipeg several months back. It was during that visit that I cornered their teacher and asked if it might be too dangerous for our kids at this time. He shrugged my concerns off. *"Our parents were asking me the same thing,"* he said. *"Why would we send our kids to Winnipeg — the Murder Capital of Canada?"*

He made his point.

I made my way from bed to the downstairs computer, and physically shaking, typed "Lufthansa" into the search engine. Nothing appeared out of the ordinary. Then I checked the *Winnipeg Free Press*, where I learned that the airplane that crashed was a Germanwings (Lufthansa-owned) flight from Spain to Düsseldorf. I was immediately relieved, but then my terror was replaced with remorse. I was feeling happy that our kids were safe, while somewhere in the world there were parents for whom the feelings of terror would not end on that day, or any day soon.

We read devastating headlines almost every day. But on March 24th, 2015 I understood how it feels to lose someone so close.

Christian came home this morning, and I hugged him more than once. They had an awesome experience, and for that I will be eternally grateful to his teachers, chaperones, billets, and many wonderful people in Israel, Jordan and Palestine that he met in his three-week odyssey.

I will forever remember the families affected by the Germanwings tragedy; I don't think I will ever be able to forget my few seconds of terror.

Paranoia

Had my usual day of driving. Kid to school, me to work. Take kid home for supper, then back to school for basketball practice. Go shopping with Roula at Polo Park. Then to Cabela's. Then Mexx. Back to school for pick up, then home. It's become routine, all this driving.

When I get up for breakfast, Olivia is still asleep. I don't see her unless I let the dog into her room. Most days her classes start after 9:30 a.m. and go through the late afternoon. When I come home, the sight of her yellow car in the driveway makes me smile — I always look forward to seeing her at the end of my workday. When the car isn't there it could be for a number of reasons. I often call her to find out where she is, which gives me, for lack of a better word — peace. Sometimes she doesn't answer right away, but often returns my call in a few minutes. Sometimes she can't, like if she is at work. Roula is pretty good at remembering Olivia's schedule, and when she gets home from work she usually fills me in.

Today the car was not in the driveway, but she did answer the phone when I called — and she was out shopping for Christian's birthday, which is tomorrow. I thanked her for answering her phone, then fell asleep. I couldn't have done that otherwise.

When she came home we were on our way out. She would be getting supper, then going out to dance classes from 9 to 11 p.m. There was an event at her boyfriend's house after that, and she would leave there at 12. I always wait up for her, and that is what I am doing at this very moment.

Usually, when Olivia leaves dance she calls home to let us know. It's mostly for me, to give me that "peace" that comes from knowing where my kids are at any given moment. Tonight she didn't call, and when I called at 11:15 she didn't answer. I managed to wait until 11:45 before calling again. Of course she was there, and thought it unnecessary to call me given the short time she'd be spending there.

I can't describe or justify the panicky feeling I get when I don't know where she is... but when the door clicks open and she says HI! (as she just did, right now) I am at total peace. Sleep will now come easy. Good night.

Red Friday

My father, William (Willy) Peters was born January 28, 1932, which would have made him an impressionable age seven at the start of World War II in 1939. He was eighth in a family that would number 11 children; one sister and six brothers before him, and one sister and two brothers after. The four oldest brothers were likely leaving by this time, the family farm too small to support all the children.

By 1940, Europe was fully engaged in war. In June, the Soviet Union was forcibly annexing Estonia, Latvia and Lithuania. Italy invaded France, and Paris fell to the Germans. And on June 24, Dad's fifth eldest brother** would turn 18 and be eligible to enlist. So he did.

That brother would experience the terrors of war firsthand – then, and in memories buried deep within, far after the war ended. And from that day forward my father would respect him like no other brother.

Peters family ancestors were among Dutch Mennonites who came from Russia to break farms in southern Manitoba in 1874. Canada's promise of land and control over culture and education strongly influenced their decision. And after experiencing persecution under the government's Russification policies they particularly appreciated Canada's offer of guaranteed exemption from military service.

They had seen what war could do.

However, the brutalities of war are easily lost on a seven-year-old boy, and little Willy dreamed of flying the bombers that trained in the southern Manitoba skies. Had he been 10 years older he would have signed up in a heartbeat. As it was he turned 18 in January of 1950, five years after the war ended. He left the farm for the city, and together with my mother Irene would raise a family of five in the post-war era. But his love and respect of the military never waned, and tears would come to his eyes **every time** he spoke of their sacrifice.

And so it didn't come as a surprise when he "joined" the military 60 years later at age 67. And off to Europe he went, with the South Alberta Armoured Regiment (SAR).

Dad's friend Omer had been unable to join his regiment for the trip, and so Dad volunteered to go in his place. He'd already accompanied Omer to a reunion in Alberta, as Omer was unable to drive. And so with the blessing of the SAR (and Mom), he bought a blue blazer and a pair of grey pants, and joined them on a tour of battle sites that would take them to England, France, Belgium, and Holland. Of course he had to explain to those who didn't notice his relative youthful appearance that he was not a WWII veteran, but most didn't seem to care; they gave him the same veneration as the others.

They walked Juno Beach, where the Canadians came ashore. They went to the Bayeux War Museum, which featured the SAR in action during their attempt to close the Falaise Gap. They placed wreathes across Normandy. They visited the graves of 3,000 Canadian soldiers (and 17 SAR comrades) in Cintheaux. And particularly significant to Dad was their tour of Belgian towns, where citizens turned out in large numbers to wave Canadian flags, and offer flowers. They even had a military flyover in their honour!

"These boys are not truly dead until they are forgotten, and the Belgian people have not allowed this to happen." –Major Danny McLeod, SAR

He loved to see the children at these ceremonies, especially the ones who help maintain the graves of their fallen heroes.

Dad always kept a respectful distance from the veterans, but they often asked him to pose with them for pictures... And of course he did not wear their distinctive beret, and stood behind them – literally, and figuratively.

During this tour of Europe, he found a way to honour his brother by purchasing a brick that would become part of a war memorial. On this brick is now imprinted the name of his brother.

They have both since passed away; Dad's brother on January 12, 2010; and "Willy" Bill Peters, on January 24, 2015. God keep them both.

** Name withheld at family request

Dad's obit

Bill passed away peacefully on January 24, 2015, just short of his 83rd birthday. He is survived by his wife of 58 years, Irene, and their children Bonnie (Doug) Jerlo, Bill (Roula) Peters, Bob (Karen) Peters, Denise (Scott) Patterson, Diane (Harold) Funk, as well as 11 grandchildren and one great grandson.

William (Bill) Peters

Bill was born January 28, 1932 to James and Aganetha Peters, the eighth of 11 children. At 19 he left home to work for CN Telegraphs, then Fort William Hydro, which led to his lineman position at Winnipeg Hydro where he worked for 23 years. Bill married Irene Robb on September 8, 1956, moving from Riviera Crescent in Fort Garry to St. Vital in 1960 where they raised their five children.

After retiring from Hydro, Bill had a successful career in life insurance. He was also successful in real estate investment and ran a tree trimming business — all to provide a better life for his family.

He became even busier in retirement, maintaining a family cottage, helping anyone who needed a truck, or tools, or tree trimming, or a listening ear. He hunted birds/deer/bear, and participated in the Manitoba Metropolitan Car Club. He was active in the Manitoba Liberal Party, served on the advisory board for MP Ron Duhamel, and was appointed a director of the Crown Assets Disposal Corporation. He loved garage sales as an excuse to chat and buy things for his children or friends. He was active in the church as a Sunday school teacher, boys club leader, trustee and committee member.

Following a severe stroke in 2007 Bill went into personal care; first at Riverview, then Vista Park Lodge, and River Park Gardens, where he lived until his passing. Heartfelt thanks to all who attended to his care. Visits from his friends were especially appreciated.

A celebration of his life will be held on Monday, February 2nd, 11:00 a.m., at Bethel Mennonite Church, 465 Stafford, with viewing starting at 10:00 a.m.; interment to follow at Green Acres, No.1 Highway East at Navin Road.

Children were especially important to Bill. In his memory, please consider a donation to the Bethel Church Youth Ministry.

You were a powerful and positive influence in many lives, Dad. You were loved, and you will be greatly missed!

He was born the seventh son of the Peters family in Plum Coulee, Manitoba. They didn't know if he would survive; but placed him in a box and put him in a warm area above the woodstove.

He died just short of his 83rd birthday.

What happened in between was the remarkable life of a man who overcame life's obstacles with determination.

Within days of having the stroke that would sideline him for seven years he said to me "I have made my peace with God, and if I am going to die, I am ready. At my funeral, tell them I was different."

He was different.

He was never afraid to be outspoken. He was direct, often less than politically correct, and sometimes brutally honest. As I said to my brother the other day, you might question his method, but never his motives. He lived in black or white; no shades of grey.

He was a man of his word.

He left home at 19, determined to show his father that he could survive, and thrive, away from the farm. He worked very hard, and in a few short years had a nice car, and a small riverfront home.

When he moved to Winnipeg he lived with his brother Peter and his wife Katie. There was a beautiful young girl who lived next door. Dad said to Peter "I am going to date that girl," to which Peter said "No chance. She's out of your league." Well, their marriage lasted 58 years. Dad was the first in the Peters lineage to marry outside the Mennonite heritage, which certainly raised a few eyebrows at the time.

Together they became a solid foundation for a family that numbers 23.

He enjoyed going to garage sales quite a bit; never looking for anything he needed, rather to look for something that he thought someone else could use — which he would buy and then give away. I think Mom considered it a successful day if I talked him out of buying anything to take home.

On one of those days many years ago, and quite out of the blue, he told me that I seemed more like a brother than a son. He argued a lot with his brothers, and so this seemed to be the ultimate left-handed compliment!

Dad's legacy? His children, two brothers and three sisters who love their mom and dad and each other, and who are all probably a little more like their father than any of us would admit.

Worst New Year's Eve. Ever.

Cyndi wasn't the girl for me.

Several class pictures from Grade 7 through 12 evidence her natural beauty; her blond hair, beautiful eyes and quick smile attracted boys like flies. And for the most part they were like flies — always buzzing around and distracting her from the one boy who would have killed (OK not really) to hold her hand on the walk home from school, but would instead hold the dreaded title of "friend".

Burton would, through junior high at least, bounce back and forth as boyfriend of Cyndi or her best friend Candy with apparent ease. I always envied that. He was the kind of person to which girls gravitated. But I wasn't that kind of kid; I really had no skills in that sense, and was a third wheel on many an occasion. Cyndi in particular treated me as a brother, letting me in to her innermost thoughts and feelings. But if I ever even thought to "make a move" she'd see it coming and I'd get "the look". There was no point in going any further, and we'd start again as good friends the next day. This went on through to the end of high school.

One New Year's Eve I landed what I thought would be the most romantic of dates with Cyndi, at a house party in Norwood. I made particular effort in dressing for the occasion — nice dress pants with patent leather shoes, my best polyester disco shirt with requisite skinny leather tie, topped with a bomber jacket. Not nearly appropriate for the -25° weather, but as we were to go in my best friend Glenn's Mustang which had great heat, I was set. Glenn was going stag.

An hour and a half into the party I found myself sitting on a couch munching on cheese snacks and surrounded by Glenn's friends, mostly strangers to me. At five minutes to 12, I nervously checked my watch. My plan was, of course, the big kiss at the stroke of midnight. I'd brushed my teeth especially for this moment! Checked my cheesy mint breath and thought it would do... but Cyndi was nowhere in sight.

At one minute to 12, I nervously started to look for her. Not in the living room. Not in the kitchen. Went downstairs, and there was Glenn holding Cyndi in his arms, administering passionate mouth-to-mouth.

I was beyond devastated.

Norwood Flats was about an eight-kilometre walk from home. At -25°C and in patent leather shoes it would take me two and a half hours. They passed me in the Mustang two hours in. It was the worst New Year's Eve ever. I didn't speak to Glenn for two years.

But to Cyndi? "It's OK," I said. And we remained friends for many more years, at least until the last time I saw her, in 1994.

On being famous

Sometimes it takes hours to write a story; other times it's written in an instant in my mind and takes longer to two-finger type it than I have patience. This story is one of the latter.

This afternoon I attended a bail hearing in support of a local musician. There were so many supporters there they were forced to move it to a larger courtroom. Still, it was standing room only and those of us standing were ushered into the hallway by Security for "fire regulation" reasons. The doors were closed; we couldn't see much and couldn't hear anything. We stayed and hoped our presence would be felt.

My decision to attend was prompted by a Facebook request from an old friend and perhaps the best musician I have ever known, Steve Bell, who simply requested of those in the Winnipeg music community to "come if you can make it". I had the time. I went. And now Steve and I were standing outside the courtroom, adding to the support numbers, if nothing else.

We were catching up when *Free Press* reporter Kevin Rollason pulled Steve aside for an interview. Steve eloquently expressed the sentiments of our collective support. He is remarkably adept at putting thought into words; anyone who knows Steve knows this. I was happy to watch, not that Kevin would ask my opinion anyway.

For my American friends... You can look up Steve Bell on Wikipedia. He is among the best-known Christian musicians in Canada and is an accomplished songwriter and record producer. Bell now has 17 albums to his credit (Yes, 17!). Among his many awards are two Junos (the Canadian equivalent of an American Music Award).

I hadn't seen Steve in quite some time, and we caught up on family and work. Steve has just released an amazing CD/book package *Pilgrimage,* and an independent documentary on his career has been released as well, posing the question those who know him wonder, "Why isn't Steve even more famous?"

Eventually we both had to leave, and Steve offered me a ride back to work. Steve said his goodbyes. We walked together to the elevator. The door opens, and there is one man centered at the rear. We enter. The doors close and he looks at Steve, then fixes his eyes on me. His eyebrows narrow. "You look familiar" he says.

I am in the Law Courts elevator with a Canadian institution, and he recognizes me! I'm thinking maybe he has seen me in the *Free Press,* or on a website. A lot of people know me from St. Boniface Hospital; maybe he works there, I supposed. "I'm Bill Peters," I said. Then doing what is only polite, I turned to introduce Steve to the stranger on the elevator, who interrupted:

"He's Steve Bell, I already know who *he* is."

High school fight

It started with an innocent comment — a thought my high school buddies all shared — but it was me who thought it "out loud" in the cafeteria. And once out and repeated, it was impossible to retract.

"How did that guy attract such a beautiful girlfriend?"

There would be no disagreement with that statement, on that day almost 40 years ago, or even to this day. It's unnecessary to name names; anyone who shared a high school class with me would know exactly who I am talking about. And if you are one of those people, you may not know something that happened as a result of my indiscretion…

There were few secrets at Dakota Collegiate, and confrontation with the offended party was inevitable. He was small in stature, yes, but his reputation as a vicious fighter preceded him. I on the other hand had never really been in a street fight in my life — my experience was limited to a one-punch hockey fight when I was 12 — so I suppose one could say that I was undefeated…

When a few days had passed without incident I thought it was over. I was wrong.

There would be a dance that Friday night, and I would attend "stag", as we said in those days. I played in a band back then, and often watched and learned as more seasoned pros took to the stage. I believe that night it was Harlequin, though it could have been Three Penny Opera; both excellent bands and equally immaterial where this story is concerned — the point being I was not with anyone, and sat alone at the top of the gym bleachers. And so there was no escape (and no backup) when he sat beside me and challenged me to a fight.

There could be no winner. It would have gone two ways: He wins, and I am beat to a pulp in front of the school. I win, and I am shamed for beating a much smaller guy. So I came up with a third plan. The conversation went something like this:

"I hear you called me a little punk. You're dead, Peters. You want to fight me? Outside!" he said.

"I am not going to fight you," I said.

"Are you afraid of me? Chicken?"

I managed to look directly into his eyes, and mustering all the bravado and courage I could, said "No. But I am afraid of what could happen. I am bigger than you, stronger than you. You don't know me, do you? I know this much, you would lose. You might even die. And I would feel horrible. I don't need that."

For reasons I don't understand, he just walked away. I never spoke to him again.

But I did speak with his girlfriend at our class's 10-year reunion. She dismissed any inquiry as to what happened with "him", but she did say to me "I should never have gone out with him. It was a waste of my high school time. But he was the only one who ever asked me out."

Olivia's grip

Parenthood is among the most difficult yet rewarding challenges of life. For me, it began December 18, 1994, in an aura of wonder and naïveté.

"I think it's time."

The ride to Victoria Hospital was silent; the enormity of what was to happen (later the next day, as it turned out) weighed heavy on our minds. The baby room had been prepared, and meticulously fitted and wallpapered. Supplies purchased. Appointments made, doctor's orders followed. Books read. Name list whittled down to two for each sex. Come what may, we were as ready as we could be, and yet not at all. We jumped willingly down the rabbit hole together.

"She's perfect."

Left alone with Olivia within minutes of her birth, I was, perhaps for the first time in my life, dumbfounded... speechless. She was placed in an incubator; perfectly silent, alert eyes wide open. I had no idea what I was supposed to feel in that moment; she was, in all ways imaginable, a perfect stranger. And so I, rather awkwardly, introduced myself.

"Hi. I am your Dad." Yes, these were the actual first words I spoke to my daughter.

Surprisingly, I didn't (perhaps couldn't) feel any kind of emotion at that time. I asked a nurse if it was safe to touch her — to hold her hand. "Of course" she said. Then Olivia's tiny grip on my finger opened my heart, and thus began the lifelong education on the incredible gift of fatherhood.

That was 26 years ago tomorrow.

In the years since, well... life happened. Christian completed our family two years later. There was school, music lessons, sports, dance, family holidays, and the highs and lows of life. But this morning, 26 years to the day after that short trip to the hospital, I am remembering the first two years and two months of fatherhood... when it was just the three of us, and I was over the moon with pride at being the father of such a beautiful daughter.

I particularly recall showing up at Mom and Dad's for Christmas dinner only a week later, and being overly protective of family who insisted on holding her. Her giggles. The joy she brought to her Pappou, and particularly Yiayia, who stayed with us until a routine was established. Baths in the kitchen sink. Mickey, our cat, marking her territory at the arrival of the intruder. (I will spare the details.)

Pool time on the deck while Roula made supper. Stroller walks in River Heights. Dressing her up in colourful dresses, especially for Easter. Reading stories, singing silly made-up songs, and trips to the library. Bundling her up in winter for sleigh rides. And her joy, pride, and ownership of her baby brother. All priceless memories.

From the beginning Olivia has been establishing a solid foothold in my heart; never so evident until the day she left to pursue PhD studies. I couldn't, can't say goodbye. It was, of course, life playing out as it should and as we planned. But it was so much harder than I imagined!

But this morning I particularly remember the feeling of anticipation those years ago, when we made the drive to Victoria Hospital. And I am filled will happy memories, and anticipation of so much more to come. Happy Birthday Olivia. You are the best. I love you THIS much!

—Dad

Hacking (cough)

Sony Pictures recently produced *The Interview*, a comedy starring Seth Rogen and James Franco that depicts a fictional assassination attempt on North Korean dictator Kim Jong Un. Sony was subsequently hacked, "likely internally" according to the story, though my Facebook news feed says US Officials have proof that the Korean government is behind it.

On *Entertainment Tonight,* Whoopie Goldberg said that if North Korea produced a movie about the assassination of the president they'd be pissed, but she didn't think the US would stoop as low as that. I don't know about that, Whoopie.

Hiroshima, non-existing weapons of mass destruction, and government-approved torture spring immediately to mind.

Freedom of Speech and the Right to Bear Arms in the USA has produced a culture of "say what we want, do what we want" — to the point that the government is now positioning itself to wage war against North Korea, using Rogen/Franco film as leverage.

When the ET report said "likely internally" I assumed they meant the hack came from inside Sony Pictures. Now I am not so sure.

The physics of poop

We lived in a small house in River Heights for the first seven years of our married life — marked (with the exception of the birth of our kids) by the uneventful passage of season. We were two young marrieds just getting by and saving for the future.

I would come home after work each day, park in the detached garage, close the door, and re-enter the yard through the gate in our white picket fence. The winter frost would heave, and the gate wouldn't close; no matter, it would be left open for the season. There were no security issues then, though we did have our barbecue stolen off the deck one summer... a story for another time.

Alongside the garage was the sidewalk to the back door of our house. Through the winter it was meticulously kept clear of snow; a necessity to maintain traction in my leather dress shoes.

But on one particularly sunny day, in -30° temperature, a strange phenomenon occurred. On a 20-foot span of sidewalk — as if placed by aliens — several small evenly spaced chunks of thoroughly frozen dog poop. And not the natural curly-cue twisties... these were sliced evenly and professionally!

In the yard, no evidence of canine trespass. No tracks whatsoever. Nothing in the back lane either. Just chunkettes of pre-sliced poo, nothing more.

To my right, a 30-foot expanse of virgin snow, with a slight upward drift to the fence. In front of me, an obstacle course of poop. And to the left, the white stucco wall of the garage. With one small brown mark. My eyes adjusted. Then another mark, and another.

On the neighbour's side of the fence, a new parking spot had been cleared in the back yard. The arc of the snowblower had been set perfectly to send the snow over the fence into my back yard. No problem with that, but when your dog's frozen poop hits the fan, well... the physics of projectile poop take over.

But it's nothing that a hockey stick and a sense of humour can't cure. Sorry about those brown marks on your garage, Rob!

Where's Christian?

Those two words used to inspire panic and raised my blood pressure a few points. Roula would say this to me at least once a day and the result would be the same each time. Inside the house, at the mall, at the park... the location didn't matter. One time when he was two we were getting ready for work and Roula couldn't find him. I ran outside, then to the furnace room and the crawl space; I was sweating bullets. Started over again from his bedroom, then Olivia's, then ours. I had an Adidas gym bag on the bed, and just as I turned to run downstairs the handle jiggled — only slightly. He was giggling inside.

These days the answer to that question is complicated by school events, work, baseball, and a myriad of other ways he can seem to disappear. Having said that, I am more panicked by Olivia (or Christian) coming home late from a party, or dance, or whatever. I wait up every time, just like my mom did for me. And it isn't getting any easier.

That is why it was particularly annoying, while relaxing at the computer just now, to hear "Where's Luna?" from upstairs. Not in my room, says Olivia. Or Christian's. Not sleeping on my bed. Not in her window seat in the living room. Certainly not downstairs with me. Not forgotten in the back yard, or accidentally caught in the garage. Not answering to her call as usual. I sprinted outside and called her name — somewhat sheepishly as the neighbours are out and they know we always keep her on a leash. It's embarrassing to lose your dog!

Then Christian pokes his head out the door and says "She was sleeping under your bed, Olivia."

Always the last place you look. Sigh.

Finding Jesus

Went to the Forks Market for lunch with Joseph and Rob. Nice walk on a sunny day, and I had perhaps just a tinge of sweat on my brow as we crossed the bridge over the Assiniboine River from St. Boniface. I was looking forward to the respite of Market A/C when I first saw Jesus.

Obviously, not the *real* Jesus.

The likeness, at least to standard Bible artwork, was uncanny. It felt like we'd walked onto a movie set. His light blue eyes fixed on me (I suppose I was the one staring) and he invited us to join him in about 20 minutes for his presentation "Truth? What is Truth?" at the Oodena Celebration Circle amphitheatre. I explained that we were just going for lunch and might join him later. "That would be great" he said. "I hope to see you then." And we parted ways.

Sitting in the air conditioned comfort of the Forks Market I was enjoying my fish and chips and the conversation of my workmates, though I must admit I kept thinking of our "Jesus encounter". We came up with a few things we could say when we got back, like "I found Jesus — He's always in the last place you look." and "I spoke with Jesus at the Forks; he recommends the fish." "We can't go to your presentation, but we know you'll forgive us." Stuff like that. Borders on blasphemy, I know...

So we finished our lunch and started for work. The lines kept flowing — "Have you seen Jesus? No really, have you? He's here at the Forks." Approaching the bridge I mused that I'd really lost a great photo op. After all, how many selfies have been taken with Jesus? We decided we'd go find him and ask for a picture. We indeed found Jesus, in an animated conversation with an audience of one.

In our brief conversation we learned that this young man — "Call me Christian," he said — was attempting to live his faith by presenting the Sermon on the Mount; a collection of sayings and teachings of Jesus emphasizing teachings found in the Gospel of Matthew (chapters 5, 6 and 7). He was earnest and sincere. His presentation is given while standing on a wooden box, to anyone who will listen.

"I gave one presentation in Osborne Village" he said. "Homeless people surrounded me, swore at me and gave me the finger. I told them that we all have rough patches in our lives and that it is important never to give up on ourselves. Then I offered them a hug. There was hesitation, but they all accepted a hug from me and went away without any further issues. It was kind of magical. It never quite goes the way you expect and it has been quite a learning experience. For everyone."

We saw Jesus all right, at least through the eyes of one "Christian". I have tremendous respect for anyone who tries as hard as this to live by their ideals.

Finding Jesus, Pt. 2

@jesusonabox is a young man exploring his faith by delivering the Sermon on the Mount while dressed as Jesus, standing on a box. I met him at the Forks Market and promised to see his 20-minute presentation some day. Today was that day.

Delayed by the threat of rain at 11:00 a.m., he postponed his performance to 3:00 p.m. at Memorial Park — currently ground zero for a campout drawing attention to murdered and missing Indigenous women. Friendly folk with a serious agenda, it was questionable whether they'd be receptive to hearing the Good News. I arrived promptly at three o'clock, expecting "Jesus" to be setting up his box. He was nowhere to be seen.

I circled the camp, taking every opportunity to peek through the 20-odd tents to see if he was there. They looked back curiously. I planted myself by a park bench and decided to wait until 3:30, thinking maybe he got caught in traffic or that his car broke down. "What kind of car would Jesus drive?" I thought...

He appeared somewhat sheepishly, obviously glad to see me waiting there. He'd been there all along — explained he'd been getting up the nerve to get out of his car; nervous about the reaction he'd provoke from this particular audience. He questioned whether it was the right thing to do. He said later that it was the sight of me waiting that gave him the confidence to go on with the show.

He put down his box and went among the 15 or so people who were sitting in open tents around fire pits. He first approached a 30-something man on a bike; placed his hand on his shoulder and calmly introduced himself. The guy just about jumped out of his skin — rode by me saying "That guy is crazy!" Others welcomed him into their tent, nodding and listening as he asked them to attend his presentation. Most make excuses for not attending, or said "We'll see."

At first, I watched from a distance. But as most seemed comfortable with him around (pretty much indifferent, actually) I decided to introduce myself and ask what they thought of their visit from "Jesus". "He's not crazy," one of them said. "He's actually kind of nice." Another rebuffed him with the comment "It's good to meet the enemy." He replied, "I hope that is not the case and we can be friends." Tough crowd to read.

Actually, during his walkabout he did much more listening than talking. These people are hurting in so many ways, and they seemed to appreciate his friendly and concerned manner. Even so, he managed to attract only six people to his sermon, including me.

This "Sermon on the Mount" was delivered by a kind and concerned, passionate man. The words "Blessed are the meek, for they shall inherit the earth." was particularly delivered with conviction. He then looked directly at me. "Blessed are those who hunger and thirst for righteousness, for they shall be satisfied." He's good.

People came and left, sometimes shaking their heads. A man with bent legs and two canes literally dragged himself to the assembly — an Elder ran to him and set up a lawn chair so he could sit down. Two stayed for the entire sermon; he recognized them as street people who'd harassed him a few weeks back in Osborne Village. This time they listened, and "Jesus" (I still don't know his name) told them they'd been on his heart since then. They were visibly moved.

Before I left he thanked me for coming. "I'm not sure I would have had the nerve to do this had I not seen you waiting. I think there is a reason you waited for me — a bigger purpose to this whole thing."

Maybe. But I made him laugh when I told him I had to get going — "I'm taking my daughter to see a Broadway show tonight and do some father/daughter bonding. It's called "Wicked". I looked as he drove off. I think it was a Suzuki.

911 memorial

My dad has been in personal care for over six years now, but he regularly makes an appearance at the strangest of times and places.

Roula and I were in New York City last month, and our first visit was to the 911 Memorial site. There are two reflection pools with the names of all the people lost in the destruction of the towers engraved around the perimeter. We had 30 minutes to walk around; not enough to see everything but certainly enough to soak in the somber atmosphere. I surreptitiously shot a photo of a man praying at one of the fountains; he was in this position (see photo) for several minutes. When he stood I went over to him and asked if he knew someone who had died in the twin towers. He said "no", and then went on to explain that he was a firefighter in France. "These are my brothers" he said. "I just felt I needed to come here to pay my respects."

Some would think it odd to approach a stranger — obviously in deep, emotional thought. My dad would have seen this as an opportunity to make a friend and learn something new, and so now do I.

Thanks for that, Dad, and Happy Father's Day in advance. I will be away on a motorcycle trip to South Dakota next week, looking for new adventures.

In a New York state of mind

We checked the map a few times to make sure we'd selected the right subway route from Manhattan to Coney Island. There are at least four different ways to get there, and you never know where the map will lead you or what path you might choose to take.

So we took the D-Train. Lots of tourists like us, with maps out or tucked in back pockets. I felt as "at home" as a Winnipegger can be on a subway; though we have nothing like this at home (understatement), I have experienced the Toronto subway system and New York's is not much different.

Of course once we left Manhattan it was a different story altogether. No tourists on this leg of the trip — just sleepy Brooklynites, perhaps on their way home from a night shift. I was mesmerized by the tenement housing and endless graffiti outside the window, and eventually lost track of the comings and goings of people at the stations, until there were four of us.

Roula and I sat face-forward in the middle of the car. There was a woman in the far right corner with her back to the window, and a man who I had not previously noticed. He stood across from the woman, though there were plenty of seats. He held the railing with both hands above his head, and was rocking steadily back and forth, in a manner reminiscent of Dustin Hoffman's autistic "rain man". The woman opposite held a steady gaze at the floor. Roula did the same.

At the next stop the woman left our car and immediately entered another. The doors however did not close and the man, after a delay message from the conductor, was now pacing near the door. Roula stood up and walked toward him, only a few steps really, briefly looked at a subway map, and returned to her seat. "CLOSE, BITCH!" the man yelled, and kicked at the door. He returned to his stance, rocking for a tense few seconds before the doors indeed closed, and we jerked forward again. When we were up to speed, he turned toward us. And with his gaze fixed on Roula and his hands moving from rail to rail, he walk/stumbled across the car towards us...

I had no idea what I was going to do, but I swear I was ready to do it. The man stopped a foot away from us, bent forward at the waist, and was eye-to-eye with Roula. He paused, and then said "I saw you looking at the map. Do you need directions?" When Roula said "No thanks, we're good." he returned to his previous location, and got off at the next stop.

Like I said, you never know where the map will lead you, or what path you might choose to take.

Learning to help

He tried his best to miss the car. Leaning his Harley hard to the right, I thought he had a chance. My two-second prayer barely left the ground when his left leg caught the rear bumper of the station wagon running a red light. He went down hard and his leathers brought him to a crumpled stop while the bike slid through the intersection. I was directly behind with wife and kids in the car. I pulled over quickly and ran through traffic to the man lying in the middle of Lagimodiere and Regent. His leg was badly broken mid-femur; his ankle came to rest at an ungodly angle near his coat pocket. He looked directly at me as I knelt beside him and said "I think my leg is broken"...

I grew up in South St. Vital with lots of neighbourhood kids. In August of 1968 (I was eight years old) it wasn't unusual for as many as a dozen of us to be outside playing in someone's yard, and as the Braun family had the biggest swings we were usually there. My memories of one particular evening stand out; it was a cool fall afternoon and Vernon Braun had the task of removing potato bugs from the vestiges of their summer garden. We were invited to help. Some were gullible enough to accept this offer of exciting adventure — or at least I was. Vernon carried a coffee can that we dropped the bugs in. In the bottom of the can — a quarter inch of gasoline from the lawnmower to keep them from crawling out. My attention span limited, I quickly lost interest in favour of a small wood fire started in the middle of the lawn and settled into a semicircle of kids, all wearing t-shirts and shorts, next to Vernon's younger brother Tim.

At nine years, Tim was one year older than me, and with no one my age in the neighbourhood, he was one of my closest friends. We spent countless hours on the aforementioned swings or in his tractor tire sandbox. We pushed each other around on wagons. We played hide and seek. In the winter we spent hours playing in his basement with road race cars. Tim's mom taught Daily Vacation Bible School and baked buns, and I loved being there. If I had a second mom in the neighbourhood it was Mrs. Braun. Or maybe Mrs. Lewer. The fact was, we were one large family in our neighbourhood and we were all looked out for, and after, by the parents that settled in our neighbourhood. Which made the fallout of what happened next bother me for years to come — after Vernon, with a flick of the coffee can and its buggy contents, unintentionally set Tim on fire.

My memory plays the scene in slow motion. I reacted to the ball of fire by repeatedly somersaulting backwards; each revolution imprinting a split second of terrifying memory, vivid to this day. First, we all instinctively catapult backward. Then Tim is standing, both bare legs ablaze. And then he his running past the fire toward Vernon. Then past, while Vernon screams at him to "Stop, drop and roll." We all knew that from school, but it never occurred to any of us that we would one day be faced with that decision. Tim didn't remember this lesson either, and was eventually forced to the ground by Vernon, who doused the blaze with dirt recently laid to level the yard. By then the gas fire had taken its toll with first, second and third degree burns. And by the time the fire was out they were the only two left in the yard. Everyone there, perhaps instinctively, returned to the safety of their homes. Including me. If memory serves I watched TV; distancing myself from the horror of the event and the possibility of being held accountable in some way.

Tim would tell me years later that the intense pain of his burns would not begin until his mother and brother put him into a cold tub of water. He would eventually be taken to the hospital by his father, not yet home from work. He would also remember, as I did, that when he turned to go inside we had all vanished. Like a magician's trick — a ball of flame and we were gone.

I visited Tim when he was released from hospital. He was bandaged from foot to hip on one side, foot to knee on the other. The pain was still evident and would be for weeks with the changing of his bandages. For years actually... Tim still bears the scars of the third degree burns to this day.

First on the scene beside the injured motorcyclist, I really had no idea what I was going to do. "I think you are right," I said, in reference to his obviously broken leg. When, thankfully, a nurse appeared and took over from me, I coordinated traffic and stood the motorcycle up so the gasoline would stop leaking from the damaged tank. I stayed until the ambulance came and helped load the motorcycle onto a trailer. It was a full 90 minutes until I returned to the car. "What have you been doing all this time?" my wife asked.

"Nothing. Just helping," I said, adding "I needed to stay."

Living through the kids

My personal sports career highlight was playing for the St. Vital Victorias AA hockey team for three years; one as a forward and two as a goalie. I think the best we ever did was just shy of a .500 season.

Fortunately, in sports, I get to live through my son now.

His varsity basketball team at Westgate Mennonite Collegiate just won the city AAA championship and will be competing in the provincials next weekend. Many of those kids won the city championship in AAA volleyball this year as well. They are an excellent group of boys in many ways, and he will miss playing with many of them when they graduate and he becomes a senior. Next year's group is very promising as well, and he will step into a larger role which will be exciting. Already looking forward to that!

He gave up hockey this year to become involved in high school sports, and I must admit I miss it at times. The last three years his AA team has made it to the city finals, and won twice. In the summers in between he focused on baseball, playing on two city/provincial champion AAA baseball teams. He has also played in two national championships where he has received several game star and MVP honours.

He plays men's league soccer in his spare time, plays guitar and drums equally well, and French horn in the high school concert band. He sings. He bugs me to take him snowboarding in the mountains, and tonight (on the way home from soccer) said bicycle ice cross would be fun to try. Lacrosse would also be nice to try.

He wears me out, at times. As they say, be careful what you wish for!

Making lemonade

I've worked almost 25 years at St. Boniface Hospital Research Centre, and in that time I have had many photographic assignments. In the early days they were all met with nervous enthusiasm; I had to prove myself capable of providing quality photography or they would outsource. My post-college job experience gave me plenty of experience shooting inanimate subjects like motorhomes at Triple E (and many of the students at South Winnipeg Technical Centre), but portraiture, or candids, were a challenge.

So when I was told I'd be shooting the Prince of Wales I was terrified.

There were to be two photographers. One would follow the Prince through various areas of the Hospital and shoot posed pictures with some of the staff as well as patients. The other was to stake out the best location in the Hospital foyer and shoot the unveiling of a plaque. The latter would be my job.

How hard could it be? I had the best of equipment at the time — a medium format Bronica with a portrait lens, and a Metz flash that could brighten the entire foyer. I selected 100 ASA film for the tightest grain; even had two 120mm film backs. I went over my settings several times. Measured distances and double-checked against the settings on the flash. I was pumped and I was prepared!

That is, until I arrived at the foyer. It was absolutely packed with people.

It is amazing how people will accommodate someone with a big camera. The seas parted for me somewhat, as I told them I was the "Official Photographer". Of course I really wasn't, but the guilt from saying so dissipated when I received a polite wave from Sister Jacquie

St-Yves of the Grey Nuns — beckoning me to join her close to the ceremonial stage. "Would you be sure to get a picture of Charles and me?" she politely asked. This would become my mission.

As I raised my camera to pre-focus, I caught the attention of the Royal Footman — who would affect all of my preparation with one command: "No flash photography." It was not a suggestion. So in a panic reflex I popped the flash off the camera and into my camera bag. He turned his attention elsewhere. I had been handed lemons.

100 ASA film is great for low-grain pictures given enough light — which the flash would have provided easily. Light in this particular room was provided by fluorescent bulbs — not only insufficient, but the wrong colour for daylight-balanced film. I started to sweat... I'd made a promise to a Nun!

Prince Charles swept through the room quickly, and I decided to go for broke. I opened up the lens to allow as much light as possible, set my shutter speed to 60, and tried to find him through the crowd of unusually tall people. It was near impossible. Suddenly he recognized Sister Jacquie and came over to shake her hand and exchange pleasantries — with his back squarely facing me. I couldn't have been closer to the action!

Unfortunately, that was the problem — I was TOO close, and couldn't possibly move back far enough to take a decent picture. It was either him or Sister Jacquie; I couldn't get both in the frame. I did manage one shot with his shoulder in the foreground and the Sister smiling upwards at him. And grainy as it was, she did appreciate the picture as well as the effort.

It seemed like an eternity. Prince Charles was literally inches away, but so squarely facing in the opposite direction as to make a recognizable shot impossible. I looked at his perfectly tailored suit and coiffed hair. I started to think about Princess Diana, and what she might have seen in him... Then I found myself staring at, of all things, his ears. Probably the most caricatured ears in the world...

Lemonade, after all!

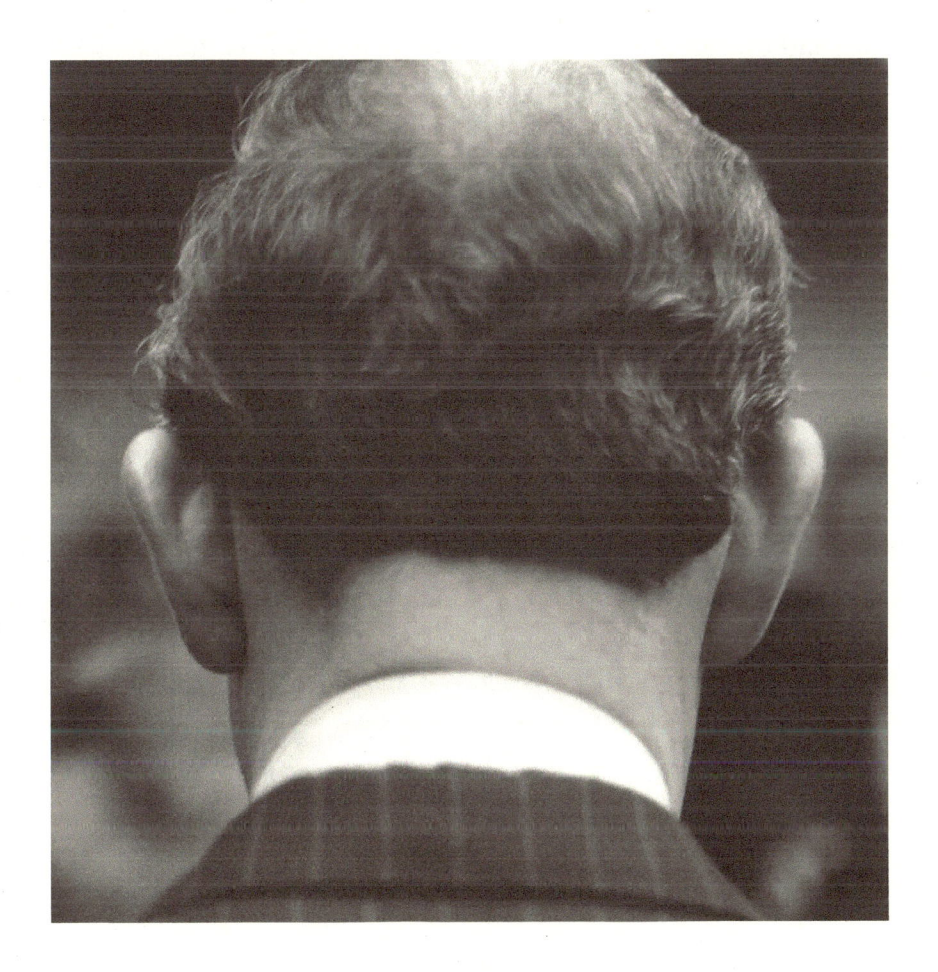

My Robbie

I was raised in a brand new house on the outskirts of Winnipeg, in the southern suburb of St. Vital, back then known as "the boonies" or "the sticks". We had perhaps a dozen neighbours — an eclectic mix of ethnicities, ages and stages in life.

Roberta "Robbie" Lewer

Looking back some 40 plus years later, it was in many ways an idyllic setting. We rode bikes, raided gardens, had paper routes, and played hide and seek until bedtime. We survived long hot summers and cold harsh winters. We played road hockey in the winter, and learned to skate on a swamp. Horses and wayward cows were not uncommon. We used the Braun's swings because they were taller, and played in their sandbox made from a tractor tire. Chorney's house smelled of holopchi. Ross MacClay practised bagpipes with his bedroom window wide open. Mr. Wiens had a naughty calendar in his garage. The MacRae's had no kids, but made a daily walk through the neighbourhood with their husky on a leash, the only ones to do so. Every family had a dog, and they all ran wild through the neighbourhood. In the winter they chose to poop *en masse* in our back yard. My job was to clean it up in the spring.

Across the street lived the Lewers, a family of four. Bob Lewer worked for CP Rail and was pro-union. Flo was a stay-at-home mom in the early years, and arranged flowers later in life when they bought a florist shop. Glenn (two years my senior) was a skinny kid with two sets of front teeth, and always seemed to have the coolest toys. We called each other every Christmas morning to ask "What'd you get?" I most always felt short-changed, though in retrospect that was never the case. Finally, there was Roberta, or "Robbie" as we called her. Glenn's older sister by five years, she was what we used to call... I can't even write it. Today they say mentally challenged.

Robbie loved kids. We were all hugged and kissed regularly, despite Mrs. L's pleadings not to. She was hard to understand, but we all smiled and shrugged our way through. I never thought of her as anything other than different. We were all different in our own way. My memories of Robbie are all positive. I remember how she loved Tom Jones and Engelbert Humperdinck records. She played them all the time...

I lost track of her over time. I'd heard she moved into a group home; a difficult but necessary move for the long-term. She lived apart from her parents with growing independence, and when Mr. Lewer died some five years ago their wisdom became more apparent to me. When Mrs. Lewer died two years ago…

Yesterday I went to pick up my son from a school play rehearsal. I arrived early at the theatre, located within the Deaf Resource Centre. While shaking off the cold and stamping the snow from my boots I looked up and there she was — walking with the aid of a walker, stooped somewhat and with greyer hair — my Robbie.

Any set of good friends can catch up — even after years — in a matter of minutes. This was no different. The familiarity of her speech, no better in so many years, was a gift from the past. Her smile at recognizing me was absolutely priceless and brings tears to my eyes just thinking about it. And introducing her to my son brought absolute joy to my Christmas season! I told him "This is my other big sister". She insisted on hugging us both. One of those moments in time. Wow.

I have to leave now to pick him up at the theatre. I hope she's there again, so we can visit a bit more. Time goes by so quickly.

Only waiting

I was shooting B-roll in Palliative Care; carrying heavy equipment and on a tight deadline. An elderly patient bluntly asked me, "Why are you here?"

"I'm with Research," I responded, evading the question.

"What are you searching for?" he demanded.

I, tired and impatient, hadn't the time. He, quite literally, had the rest of his life.

I put my equipment down. "I'm looking for a shot that represents this ward," I said.

He pointed over my shoulder, so I turned around. At the end of the hall, past a dozen or so resident rooms, the morning sun shone through the window and reflected brightly, almost blindingly, off the polished tile floor. I had taken a few steps, when the irony of walking "toward the light" on this particular floor brought a smile to my face.

I turned to thank him. My equipment remained, but he was not there. He had returned to his room, to resume waiting.

Westminster chat

I walked my son to Westminster Church; he and his French horn buddies were opening for a symphony event. I walked out the front doors to the peal of the tower bells with an hour to kill. Felt inspired. The slow-falling snow and relatively mild temperature (-10°) made for a peaceful walk in the Westminster/Sherbrook area; lots of trendy bistros with students using wireless to study while sipping their trendy toddies and macchiatos — in stark contrast to my unplowed path just feet away.

At the end of the block a lone figure stood waiting for the light to change. She turned toward me and asked if I had change. I suppose she caught me somewhat off guard and after fishing through my keys I awkwardly said "Sorry, no." She seemed to appreciate my effort though, and politely said "That's OK."

The light changed and we crossed together. More delis and bistros. I started to feel a presence come up behind me.

"Are you from here?" she asked.

I suppose it looked like I was looking for a place to eat but the fact was I was feeling guilt knowing I could afford to eat at any of these places, while this woman apparently could not. I told her that I was just going for a walk while waiting for my son. "I live here, but I'm not from here" she said, and thus started a 30-minute conversation.

Marguerite (same name as the foundress of the Grey Nuns for whom I have worked this past 24 years) cleared the snow from a bus stop bench and beckoned me to "visit". Age 50, mother of a boy (28) and girl (22) with a grandchild on the way. Originally from Rankin Inlet, lived in Whitehorse, then Selkirk for a few years, then Winnipeg. "I love this neighbourhood," she said. Unemployed but looking for a job. Short and heavyset with a wide toothless grin, she wore a home-knit toque and a maroon parka. Reminded me of an Inuit doll.

Her mother, a seamstress, died a few years ago; her father, aged 71, just recently "presumed dead". Presumed? What? I had to ask...

A few weeks ago her son had taken him fishing by snowmobile in the Whitehorse wilderness. On their return the father fell off the sled he was pulling behind. When he noticed some miles later that his grandfather wasn't there he had to make a choice; go back and risk running out of gas, or continue to Baker Lake and send back a search party. He chose the latter and his grandfather has not been found.

We spoke further of our love and concern for our kids, fishing, Churchill and polar bears, and the beauty of snow flaked and mild weather. She smoked a couple of sidewalk butts and apologized for her "addiction". She helped a woman with her bus route questions, and we both shook our heads at three high school girls who ran by in miniskirts. Presumably between bistros.

At 6:55 p.m. I told her I had to go meet my son. She stood with me and I gave her a $5 bill with the explanation "I said I had no change, you didn't ask me about this." I said it with a smile and she got the joke. I wished her Merry Christmas and she said "You too!" She gave me a big hug and said she hoped she'd see me again sometime.

I walked a few feet, and turned to face her. *"You probably will,"* I said. *"I love this neighbourhood."*

Young boy's dream

In 1973 a young boy and his father sat in the front row of the Winnipeg Centennial Concert Hall, thoroughly enjoying a Buddy Rich concert. The boy dreamed that one day he'd perform on that stage.

Forty years later, he would achieve that dream, if only through his beautiful daughter, singing with Prairie Voices and the Winnipeg Symphony Orchestra.

It was all he imagined it would be!

Squeeze your bum?

I walked south Sherbrook this afternoon. Stopped to chat with an Indigenous woman who'd asked me for a quarter. Talked about her kids (two, aged 23 and 21) and her upbringing in Nelson House on a trapline. Showed me her scar from leg surgery required for a bad fall, the reason she couldn't work. Told me the quarter was for a Tall Boy, and laughed when I asked her if she meant beer. Bought her a slice of pizza a block away; she tried to hold my hand on the walk, but I told her my wife would be jealous.

Slice of pizza in one hand, she asked *"Can I squeeze your bum?"* Again I politely declined. I told her it was time for me to continue my walk and she said "Thanks for the pizza." This is how I entertained myself while waiting for my son's volleyball practice to finish.

The secret to marriage

Twenty-second wedding anniversary today. Celebrated in our traditional fashion... Roula went for a run, then out for coffee with a friend. Then she spent the rest of the day sorting paperwork. I took Christian for a haircut, painted the front window frame, went to a memorial service, then to Christian's doubleheader. Just got home and she's already had supper. I am starved, but there's nothing in the house.

THAT's how we have made it this far.

Mementos

Bottom of the last inning, down 4 to 2 with one out and one on base, Christian hits a 380-foot home run to tie the game. After the game his coach comes up to me, and after scribbling something on the ball in his hand he asks, "You keep mementos like this?" Those are the things a dad never forgets.

Cheaper. Much cheaper.

Anyone who thinks hockey is expensive doesn't have a kid in AAA baseball. I've spent more on cleats than skates, bats than sticks, and gloves than, well, gloves. And even more on travel and hotels. Not complaining though, like they say, it's cheaper than lawyers.

Pawsh Tidy, please

For years I've been telling my wife that we are, for all intents and purposes, rich. We have little debt, our kids are awesome, and our life is busy and full.

But this morning something happened that fully defines our achievement level in this life. In addition to ferrying the kids around to their appointments, I am off to pick up Luna the Wonder Dog from the spa, where she is having the "Pawsh Tidy"; a bath/brush/ears, face, and bum cleaning. A dog's life is certainly not what it used to be!

Cars that can fly

Me: *Yesterday I saw a beautiful 1990 Corvette for sale, loaded and in amazing condition. I could have bought that car with what I put out for you on hockey and baseball in one year.*

Son: *Yeah, but you CHOSE to have kids. That's like having cars that can fly!*

Trunks of cars

Conversation in the car tonight:

Me: *If you had $1,000, what would you buy?*

Son: *A truck.*

Daughter: *What do you need a truck for?*

Son: *You know, for friends, illegal immigrants and to move stuff.*

Daughter: *That's what trunks are for.*

Son (to me): *She thinks illegal immigrants belong in the trunks of cars. Sad.*

Miss Universe

While watching *Miss Universe* on TV...

Son: *How do they sleep in those?*

Me: *What do you mean?*

Daughter: *It's the evening gown competition... not nightgown.*

Son: *Oh.*

The ICONic last word from Stephen Eric McIntyre

Stephen Eric McIntyre

We'd just started our daily walk at St. Vital Park when a cc'd text referencing Steve's untimely passing came to Earl, with this plea:

"Please say it's a joke." Karen wrote. "WTF?!?!?!?!" Earl responded.

WILLIAM J PETERS

Karen, Earl, Steve and I have known each other since high school and beyond. Back in the day it would have been "Did you hear?" with a sideways glance in a classroom. News would spread from there, organically, by word of mouth. Yet here we are, our 64-year-old thumbs fumbling cryptic texts in disbelief at the loss of our friend.

Steve McIntyre was gone. WTF indeed.

Just one day before, Earl and I had been discussing the stages of grief, Earl having just lost a favourite uncle. I found it particularly interesting how we both went to thoughts of our last words with the departed; words now imbued with special meaning, as "the last words". These days, those words would likely be in the form of texts. And in Steve's case those words are documented as chat history:

Me: *It's coffee time, my friend.*

Steve: *Sure.*

Me: *Whenever suits. The ball is firmly in your court.*

Steve: *(Thumbs up icon)*

Thumbs up indeed, Mr MacIntyre. The offer stands.

Whenever suits.

About St. Amant

St. Amant supports more than 5,000 people in Manitoba with developmental disabilities, autism and acquired brain injury. We are a not-for-profit organization that offers a wide range of supports for adults, children and their families, such as accessible living accommodations, recreation and day programs, physiotherapy, occupational therapy, speech therapy, nutrition, dental care, pre-school autism program, respite, foster care, supported independent living and community daycare. More than 2,000 staff follow a person-centred approach and adapt to the needs of each person and each family.

Funds raised through the St. Amant Foundation support the purchase of mobility equipment and communication devices, recreational and leisure activities, accessible transportation and capital projects like renovations to living areas and community homes and fundamental support to the St. Amant Research Centre.

St. Amant strives to support Manitobans with developmental disabilities to live meaningful lives as valued members of our community, and is committed to human rights and full community inclusion.

For more information and to donate, please visit: stamant.ca/foundation/

About the Author

Bill Peters is an award-winning corporate communicator by profession; husband and father by passion; a biker, car guy, rock drummer, hockey, baseball, soccer and dance dad; and in his retirement apparently an author.

He is a lifelong Winnipegger, save for a two-year stint in the homeland of the Peters family, Winkler, Manitoba. He contends he was sent back to Winnipeg because he didn't marry, citing "too many cousins".

Bill says a side benefit of marrying his Greek-born wife Roula is that it freshened his Mennonite gene pool, which produced two beautiful kids. He adds, "I'm the only one without a degree in my family. I'm amazed they still ask me for advice. I watch home improvement shows and sports while they watch CNN. That should tell you all you need to know."

Long Stories Shortened is a compilation of over 100 amusing, sometimes poignant stories which were initially intended to pass down to his children. Encouragement from friends, family, and a healthy Facebook following has resulted in this book.

Printed in Canada